we want
EQUALITY

HOW THE FIGHT FOR EQUALITY
GAVE WAY TO PREFERENCE

C. Douglas Love

ISBN: 978-0-9891959-2-8

Published by Thinkordie.org

For those who are shouted down, ostracized, and attacked for speaking the truth but refuse to be deterred from fighting the mob; and all of those who will join them ...

Table of Contents

Preface

Equality. What a powerful word. Achieving it is a lofty goal and, to date, we've produced only a modest degree of success. Martin Luther King Jr., Alice Paul, Crystal Eastman, Harry Wu, Dietrich Bonhoeffer, Lech Walesa, and Nelson Mandela all made tremendous inroads toward this goal. However, do some research and you will find that Mao Zedong, Josef Stalin, Fidel Castro, and Adolf Hitler also spoke regularly of their goal of equality. Hundreds of books have been written about the methods, the results, and the actions of both groups. History tells us that equality is not the norm.

As the title of the book states, the long fight for equality has morphed into something the original catalysts for change wouldn't recognize. When people fought the injustices of the past century, they were demanding changes to laws that stated they were not equal. Some laws prohibited newly arriving immigrants from living in certain areas or owning property, others limited the jobs blacks and others were allowed to hold. This extended into the military for decades. Voting rights were limited by poll taxes and reserved exclusively for men. The point here is clear; the laws they were fighting against supported unequal treatment. Unfortunately, when those laws went away, the government turned a blind eye to those who maintained the practices. This is no longer the case. There is nowhere in the country today where it is legal to list a home for 'whites only,' ban women from voting, or post a job stating 'blacks need not apply.'

Now I know what my friends on the left will say, "Racism today is covert rather than overt." I completely agree, as much as it exists. Since the racism is now mostly covert, it's hard to determine how that racism leads to inequalities. There are two problems those fighting perceived inequalities face: (1) how to define equality, and (2) how to, through legislative means, achieve it.

Defining equality is difficult. As I often say, words matter. How you define what you're striving for will dictate what you're willing to do to achieve it and how you measure your success. Merriam Webster defines equality as: "The state or quality of the same measure, quantity, amount, or number as another; c: like for each member of a group, class, or society."

Based on this definition, you have to ask if this is something that can even be accomplished. Equal in 'measure and quantity' for each member of '… a group, class, or society'? Where would this work? The job market? The housing market? How about with salaries or education? Logic dictates that any effort to achieve equality will result in further inequality.

Let's take the example of a marriage. Both spouses should be equal partners in the relationship, but by the definition above, there would rarely be true equality—'measure and quantity.' If one spouse does all of the cooking and the other cleans, some will say this is equality; they are each responsible for one task. But if the spouse who does the cooking notices that it takes over an hour to prepare dinner but only 15 minutes to clean up, he may begin to complain that the arrangement is not equal.

In an effort to correct this inequality, he offers a solution. His spouse will do all of the laundry where previously they split the duties. Now that spouse, considering all of the loads that need to be washed, the many trips back and forth to the laundry room and folding and putting away of the laundry, complains that the inequality has simply shifted.

While an obvious oversimplification, the marriage example suggests an inherent flaw in 'equality for all'. There are too many variables. As difficult as it is to achieve equality in quantity, having the same measure is exponentially more difficult. During the Civil Rights movement, for example, blacks and whites each had the use of drinking fountains and schools as well as areas to sit on busses and in auditoriums, but there was a huge disparity in the measure of each. If whites and blacks both had water fountains, but the blacks' fountains were farther away, dirtier, or often broken, few would see that as equal. Also, if a white person wanted to, he could use the blacks-only areas; the opposite was not allowed.

Perhaps the better fight is for fairness rather than equality. The Merriam Webster definition for fair is: "marked by impartiality and honesty: free from self-interest, prejudice, or favoritism." This seems closer to what many demanding equality are trying to achieve. It also points to the glaring differences in the treatment of blacks during Jim Crow, regardless of any perceived equality. It's not fair to have subpar housing, subpar water fountains, or to be treated as a second-class citizen even if the laws allowing this no longer exists. Fairness, however, has its own set of challenges. It is subjective and open to a wide breadth of interpretation. Not only is it difficult to determine what's fair, the greater challenge is who gets to determine its absence or existence.

Let's use housing as an example. Everyone will agree that we all deserve a place to live. Most will even say a 'decent' place to live. But who determines what's decent? It's easy to see that living in a building managed by a slumlord with sporadic utilities, deficient appliances, and dirty, unsafe common areas is unfair. But what about a family of four living in a one-bedroom apartment, or a fifth-floor unit with no elevator, or a clean, well-appointed apartment an hour away from work in a food desert? Many will say these situations are also unfair.

Here's another housing angle. Many say owning a home is the American dream, and being denied this opportunity is unfair. Does this mean the fact that some people own, while many more rent, is a form of inequality? We hear a lot about rich versus poor. Is the fact that some people own mansions while others have small homes or condos unfair? This can go on in virtually every situation.

Even if we somehow reached a consensus on what is unequal and unfair, that would be the easier part of the fight. The bigger challenge would be how to correct it, and the social justice warriors (SJWs) are going about it the wrong way. Criminals evolve, so law enforcement has to evolve with them. There were no hacking crimes a few decades ago. Now they're prevalent, and law enforcement agencies have created whole divisions dedicated to stopping them. Those seeking 'social justice' haven't evolved. They are fighting today's issues in the same manner the Civil Rights movement was fought. They need a 21st century approach.

When laws stated that blacks were not afforded the same rights as whites; that was prima facie racism. The laws that are being opposed now are not so clear cut. In most cases, the opponents are arguing against the intent of the law rather than the letter of the law. They assume that if the outcome of the law will have a negative effect on minorities that means the law is racist. Predicting the outcome of a law is not an easy task, and the outcome is often no indication of its original intent.

Let's use voting ID laws as an example. Those fighting them argue that they are racist, an attempt to suppress the black vote. To prove the argument, they usually look to the results in areas where these types of laws have been implemented. There are too many factors that affect voter turnout, so that evidence is circumstantial. That means all of the arguments against the law would be anecdotal. They may be right about the effect on the black vote; they may not. One thing is certain; however, they'll never know if the law was proposed with racist intent. This is important because what they're actually doing is opposing a law they don't agree with, which is completely fine, but adding an unfounded racial angle to the argument; something they know will rile up some who know nothing about the law and strike fear in those endorsing it.

This is not to endorse or oppose voter ID laws. The point here is to show that using these old tactics muddies the waters of racism, and if everything is racist, nothing is racist. You'll lose some who may have joined you, and using racism as a club to strike your opponent is lazy and renders you unable to make cogent arguments. There may be strong constitutional arguments that can be made against voter ID laws, but when people decide the law has racial intent, they don't bother to look for them. A better approach would be to spend the money and effort to ensure that every person who can legally vote gets an ID. This way, it would no longer matter if the intent of the law was racist, you would have removed the discriminatory effect.

What these demands of equality really boil down to is policing thought and intent. If the president has executive authority to enforce a policy but some believe his intent is bad, should the courts be able to stop him from enforcing the policy? If one president can use executive powers to mandate something, can his successor use executive power to undo that mandate? Until recently, these things have never been in question.

Some things cannot be regulated, and if you try, the outcome will almost always be unfair to someone. Some will say they are okay with it, for the greater good. But unless everyone is okay with it, it is not equality. Taking from the rich, without their permission, to give to the poor is not equality, that's theft. In that case, why stop there? You should demand that everyone make the same salary regardless of title, industry, or workload. Anything less is, by the Left's definition, inequality.

In this book, I will discuss what many deem as the fight for equality and expose both its flaws and the blatant hypocrisy of those demanding it. I will also give glaring examples of how the baton of liberty and justice for all has been picked up by people who no longer want liberty or justice. What they want is preference and 'social justice' for some. If the original freedom fighters could see what their fight has become, they would be aghast at how those arguing under the same umbrella are regressing, not advancing, the cause.

In several places I will refer to my approach called the Logic Board. Here, to accentuate a point, instead of saying an argument is wrong I will give the opponent his argument, then go through the logical steps that follow. The goal is to allow them to see flaws in their argument rather than to dictate to them. Here's an example.

Let's say a congressman sponsors a bill making carjacking a crime with a mandatory 20 year minimum sentence. We'll also assume that 90% of the offenders are blacks. The opponents to the law say it's racist on the grounds that it disproportionately affects blacks and is an attempt to lock up black men. We'd go to the Logic Board:

If you cannot agree on the first question, stop; they are irrational. If you cannot agree on the second question, ask what the punishment should be and how we would prevent repeat offenses. The third question would be where extended discussions can be had. If this is the only disagreement, not only can a compromise be found, but it debunks the racist component, unless they are willing to argue that sentencing for crimes should be based on the race of the perpetrator and not the severity of the crime committed.

As you will see, the goal is not always to change their minds. It is to allow for better clarity, pinpoint where the differences lie, as well as where agreement can be found, and demonstrate whether the opponents are being rational or not.

We will also evaluate the claims of inequality in several areas to determine if bias and discrimination are the reasons for the inequalities. Where the findings don't support these claims, evidence will be provided along with a detailed explanation of why discrimination is not the cause of the unequal results, or why it's just a small factor in a list of things that contribute to them.

In those situations where there is bias, discrimination, or racism, we will address it directly and offer the most effective method to combat it. This will almost always be through non-governmental intervention. Looking to the government for cures to social ills is wrong. It is not their role, and we have many years of evidence that proves they are bad at it. It is better for those who are truly trying to create an equal environment to do it themselves, but watching the SJWs, it's obvious they don't know how. There is something here for them as well. Hopefully, opening their eyes to the twisted information they've been given will help them shift their approach and focus on true inequalities instead of misconceptions.

Finally, the most important goal of this book is to show that our problems are more cultural than legislative. The Left has had control of our culture for years, and has been slowly moving it in a secular and nihilistic direction. Through the media and entertainment, they've been able to deconstruct societal norms and push a political agenda. This shift has accelerated in recent years, and there's no telling how far it will go if nothing is done to quell it.

I will end by giving steps we can actively take to wake the sleeping giant within all of us. Those who see the destructive behavior but think ignoring it will make it go away. The people who allow the loudest voices to drown out civility and logic, even if they're wrong. In order to right the ship and defeat those intent on destroying the country, you have to know the enemy. This book will help you understand the truth about equality, how the Left produces inequality, how their actions are hurting everyone, and what we can do to stop it.

· 1 ·

Equality: A Brief History

*We'll be remembered more for what we destroy
than what we create.*

– Chuck Palahniuk

Human nature is flawed. From the murder of Abel at the hands
of his brother Cain, brought on solely due to jealousy, people
have acted in selfish, violent, and unfair ways. Shortly after Abel's
murder, Genesis chapter 6 verse 5 states, "The Lord saw how great
the wickedness of the human race had become on the earth, and
that every inclination of the thoughts of the human heart was only
evil all the time." Genesis 6 continues in verse 11, "Now the earth
was corrupt in God's sight and was full of violence."[1]

Sin has been with us since Adam and Eve ate of the forbidden
fruit, and will always be a part of humanity. It is probably more
accurate to say that we are constantly fighting our bad nature in
order to do good than it is to say that we are basically good and
occasionally act badly. The Bible is full of laws prohibiting bad
behavior because there is a strong temptation for people to act in
their own interests, regardless of consequences.

For those who do not want to use religion as a guide, there are
many historical examples of immoral behavior. What is most telling
is the fact that these things continued to happen, regardless of the

level of experience people gained from history. No matter how cultured societies got, or how advanced technology, science, or government became, humans continued to act according to their nature. As evidence of these flaws, we will do a quick run through history to highlight the evils that men do.

Modern man has been around for tens of thousands of years. Though we only have about 4,000 years of written word, archeological digs and other historic discoveries have given us insight into how humans lived in antiquity. Based on the weapons, helmets, shields and walled ruins we've found, we have evidence of human conflict from the beginning. It is safe to assume, however, that there were far fewer clashes in the beginning. Since the world was less occupied, people were more spread out and less likely to encounter hostiles.

The fact that most of the world's civilizations were hunter-gatherers also helped. That would soon change as people began to move to agrarian societies. While the world was vast, areas suitable for farming were much more exclusive. Add to this the fact that technology had not yet reached the point where people could survive far away from all the conditions needed to farm. This means people would begin searching for ideal land, usually near water. It was only a matter of time before conflicts ensued.[2]

CONQUESTS

Groups that settled in a particular area would claim it as theirs. Sometimes they peacefully co-existed with neighboring tribes, other times they fought for control. As populations grew, some tribes absorbed others and kingdoms were formed. The leaders exerted their strength by trying to expand. This brought them into conflict with neighboring tribes or opposing kingdoms.

Middle East

If we look at the first city-states of Mesopotamia, we see conquering from the beginning. Its major city of Kish was captured by Sargon of Akkad who made himself ruler.[3] When the last of his line died, there were revolts within the kingdom as well as invasions from without.[4] This template would repeat itself the world over for centuries, and is still continuing in some countries.

Mesopotamia was conquered by the Babylonians who were conquered by the Assyrian Empire, who later annexed the Hittites.[5] They were in and out of power with Egypt and Babylon.[6] In Greece, the Greco-Persian Wars were a series of conflicts culminating with the defeat of Persia.[7] Internally, Athens and Sparta battled in the Peloponnesian War.[8]

Macedonia, led by Alexander the Great, conquered Persia who had taken power from the Egyptian Pharaohs. He would eventually control most of the Middle East. Upon his death, the region fell into chaos as various factions fought to take control.[9] The Roman Empire emerged and was later split into two.[10]

From the beginning of the first civilization of Mesopotamia to the fall of the Ottoman Empire spanned nearly 5,000 years. In that time, the Middle East had been controlled, completely or in part, by the Greeks, Egyptians, Romans, Kushans, Babylonians, Assyrians, Persians, Mongols, Macedonians, the Byzantine Empire, and the Arab Caliphates; all conquering along the way.

Africa

Much of central and southern Africa was ruled by sacred chiefdoms. [11] The area consisted of various peoples conquering neighbors or defending themselves from others. Many Nubian kingdoms battled each other to expand their power. As Vansina, noted authority on the Oral Tradition, says, "Probably all the African kingdoms have been enlarged by conquest."[12]

Egypt controlled much of northern Africa. At their height, they extended as far south as Sudan, conquering less powerful kingdoms. However, Kush, a Nubian empire, conquered Egypt but was in turn conquered by Assyria.[13] [14] Carthage was a city-state in northern Africa, which was controlled by the Romans after the Punic Wars.[15]

Makaba II of Botswana conquered neighbors before being invaded by south Africans. The Khoi and San people of Angola were displaced by Bantu arriving from Nigeria and Niger. In western Africa, the Ghana Empire was consumed by the Malli Empire.[16]

In south Africa, growing population led to tribal empires trying to conquer each other. This gave way to the rise of Shaka Zulu.[17] "During the 1820s, the Zulu kingdom became increasingly predatory. Shaka sent the army on annual campaigns, disrupting local chiefdoms to the north and south, destroying their food supplies, seizing their cattle."[18]

Asia

China was ruled by various dynasties from the Xia dynasty in 2000 BC to the end of the Qing dynasty in 1912.[19] They, like the rest of the world, were wrought with constant uprisings with each subsequent dynasty gaining power by force. "Warfare could lead to the overthrow of a rival feudal lord and expansion of territory, but more often the aim appears to have been simple looting and the capture of prisoners. Ten or twenty or more prisoners at a time were taken to be enslaved and used for household service, as soldiers, and sometimes as victims in human sacrifices."[20]

In fact, while the Great Wall of China we see today was finally built to control its border with foreigners, it started with a series of walls built to block invasion or raids by mounted tribes and torn down to allow those in charge to demobilize armies and control the population.[21]

This changed with the Mongol Empire. From its founding, Genghis Khan wanted to increase his kingdom and amass wealth and power. At the end of the 13th century, the Mongol Empire controlled most of Asia and Eastern Europe. Similarly, India endured centuries of fighting for control with various short-lived kingdoms until the Delhi Sultanate of the 13th century. The Mughal Empire took control of northern India in the 16th century.[22]

Europe

Starting with ancient Greece, the inhabited areas of Europe were controlled by many of the groups who were in power in the Middle East.[23] These include the Greeks, the Phoenicians and the Persians. In northern Europe, the Germanic Tribes came to power in the 2nd century CE. These tribes included the Goths, Vandals, and Franks, among others. [24] They moved south, expanding their territory at the expense of the Celtic people. After the Roman Empire split, the western empire was attacked by both the Visigoths and the Vandals, while Attila the Hun attacked several areas of the eastern empire.[25]

By the 8th century, Muslims had invaded Europe and the Vikings began to rise. They used their navigational skills to extend into North Africa, the Middle East, and North America. They raided, pillaged, acted as mercenaries, and settled colonies. William the Conqueror, the Norman leader who defeated England, was a descendant of Vikings.[26]

Americas

The Olmecs were the first major civilization in what was known as Mesoamerica. They diminished, either by environmental strife or conflict, and were followed by the Mayans.[27] The Mayans and Aztecs controlled much of Mesoamerica in Pre-Columbian times. They fought wars with the intent purpose of conquering their opposition.[28][29] They remained in power until the Spanish, with help from some indigenous allies, conquered them.[30] In South America, the Incans held expansive power and, like the Aztecs, they conquered their way north.[31]

As you can see, conquering other tribes or opposing kingdoms was the norm throughout history. While some of these actions were for survival, most were motivated by greed, a thirst for power, or bloodlust. These conquests are less frequent today, but still have happened in modern history. Even after creation of the League of Nations and later the UN, countries still tried to take land by force.[32] Japan occupied Taiwan, Indonesia annexed East Timor, Saddam invaded Kuwait, and Putin attempted to invade the Crimea.[33][34][35][36] Even ISIS, in a more rudimentary way, is a land grab. Their intent is to create a new caliphate.[37]

This conquer cycle experienced a surge beginning around the 15th century, when the greed of the past was combined with advanced naval forces and cultural conflicts. We will now address the result of this phenomenon: colonialism.

COLONIALISM

The age of discovery changed the world's landscape forever. People often say Christopher Columbus was lost and is credited for finding a land where people already lived.[38] But if you look at it in their time, 15th and 16th century explorers like Magellan, Vespucci, Henry the Navigator, and others, found places no outsider had seen, connected cultures, which expanded knowledge, and found quicker routes that changed warfare and trade forever. It was an arduous undertaking and accelerated the advancement of their civilizations.[39]

The initial purpose of exploration was innocuous, the same cannot be said for the results. Had it not been for greed, cultural differences, and disease, it may have been beneficial for the people they encountered as well for the exploring nations. Unfortunately, human nature had its way. Looking back with hindsight, however, we know it was destined to fail. If tribes had been at odds for years with people who looked like them, had similar cultures, and understood their language, how could anyone expect conflicting cultures to coexist without conflict?

Colonialism differs from conquests in some ways, though the results are the same. While force was used where necessary, colonists used bribes, tricks, and advanced wealth to gain access and coerce local leaders to give them access to ports, land, labor, and resources.[40] The first European countries to colonize a foreign land were Portugal and Spain.[41] Other European powers quickly joined them. They could not allow their adversaries to have unfettered access to this new stream of revenue and resources.

Britain, France, and the Dutch challenged the exclusivity of Spanish and Portuguese exploration. They set out on their own and attacked Spanish ships in an effort to control lands to which they had laid claim. Belgium, Germany, Italy, Sweden, and Russia also expanded into foreign land.[42] At the height of colonialism, these empires would control over 80% of the world.[43] This is also where the transcontinental slave trade began. These colonies remained intact for several hundred years.

WAR

Wars have been prevalent from antiquity to modern times. While various actions can start a war, most wars fall into three categories: aggression (Germany, Napoleon, Japan, and Polk's 'Manifest Destiny'), revolution (France, Haiti, and America), and the most common: border wars.

Border wars are common because land rights are difficult to settle. In early civilizations, people were nomadic. There were no formal claims to land. If you found fertile land that was being occupied, your choices were to move along in search of other suitable land or try to settle in occupied land. Sometimes tribes peacefully coexisted. In many cases, they did not. This was a chance you had to take as your survival was at stake.

Even countries that had established land agreements had disputes. Either the parties disputed the dividing line, or accused each other of not respecting those lines. In other cases, the power who had control of the land was defeated, so new groups came in to claim that land. The Korean War, the Crimean War, and the Chaco War were all border wars. The US had border wars with Mexico, Spain, and several Indian tribes. Pakistan and India have fought no less than three border wars.

Civil wars are another common type of war. They usually come from a group feeling oppressed by the power structure within a nation and rising up. The Vietnam and American civil wars are easily the best known and bloodiest. The Colombian Conflict, Sri Lankan, Angolan, and Afghan civil wars are the longest. Some, like the War of the Roses and the Columbian Conflict, are the result of internal power struggles, while others, like Vietnam and Afghanistan, have global implications and grow into proxy wars.

While history will show that war is as old as man, with many countries born out of war, it is not something we have evolved beyond. In the last 100 years, there have been civil wars on every continent except for Antarctica.[44]

SLAVERY

Slavery is arguably man's most horrific flaw. It's also one of the most widespread. There is evidence of the practice in nearly every civilization. Those who didn't hold slaves were probably enslaved. The most common form was indentured servitude. While many volunteered their services as payment of a debt, most were treated poorly and were not released when their debt was paid.

Beginning in the 7th century, Arabs started the practice of transporting slaves as forced labor; a full 700 years prior to the transatlantic slave trade.[45] Once the transatlantic slave trade started, every prominent empire joined that practice. As David Forsythe notes, "The fact remained that at the beginning of the nineteenth century an estimated three-quarters of all people alive were trapped in bondage against their will either in some form of slavery or serfdom."[46]

When people discuss slavery in America, they rarely mention the role of Native Americans. Slavery was common before colonization, though those captured were not viewed as property. After colonization, the five 'civilized' tribes: Cherokee, Chickasaw, Choctaw, Creek, and Seminole, all owned African slaves.[47] Many also were paid to return runaway slaves to white owners. When the Civil War ended, the 1866 Indian Treaties compelled them to give their slaves full tribal citizenship. The Cherokee Nation, instead, implemented a blood descendant rule to block their benefits.[48]

Many think slavery is a problem of the past, but the practice is thriving today in various forms. *End Slavery Now* estimates that over 70 million people have been forced into one of these servile positions: domestic servitude, sex trafficking, forced labor, bonded labor, child labor, or forced marriage (This of girls under the age of 18).[49]

GENOCIDE

Genocide or ethnic cleansing is another human atrocity that has been prevalent throughout history. The best example of this is the Holocaust. Yet this has been far more common than many believe. In antiquity, the Roman siege of Carthage in 146 BC is often called the first genocide.[50] However, 250 years earlier, Athenians carried out a vicious attack on Melos.[51]

In modern times, The USSR killed millions of Pols, Kulaks, Latvians, Chechens, Kazakhs, and Ukrainians through pogroms and intentional starvation in the Holodomor.[52] Nearly two million

Armenians, Greeks, and Assyrians were killed by the Ottoman Empire, and Pol Pot's Khmer Rouge killed two million Cambodians, nearly 20% of the population.[53] [54] In Rwanda, nearly one million Tutsis were killed by the Hutu, and nearly one million Bengali Hindus were killed in Bangladesh.[55] [56] Many suggest that the Rohingya people are experiencing a genocide in Malaysia today.[57]

We can't forget the large number of people who are killed or displaced by extreme violence and poverty in their native land. I call this inadvertent genocide. For instance, since the beginning of the second Congo War, over 2 million people have been killed in five years. In 2017 alone, 1.7 million Congolese, about 5,500 per day, fled the conflict.[58] In recent years, people have fled oppression in North Korea;[59] civil wars in Syria, Afghanistan, and the Sudan;[60] [61] [62] drug cartels in Mexico and Columbia; extreme violence in Latin America;[63] and the economic collapse in Venezuela.[64]

RELIGION

Religious persecution is another common form of oppression. The methods of mistreatment have changed, but religious minorities have rarely been given equal treatment. Unlike previous empires, Constantine's Byzantine Empire and the Arab caliphates conquered with the intent of expanding Christianity and Islam respectively. This means to achieve their goals they had to suppress the freedoms of opposing religions.[65]

Jerusalem is unique in that all three major religions consider it holy land.[66] From the time of Rome's control, in the 1st century CE, to the end of the Ottoman Empire, control of the city changed many times. Each change brought with it some form of religious persecution. Jewish temples were destroyed by Muslim empires, Muslims and Jews were banned by Christian empires, and Christians were slaughtered by Jews.[67][68] The Fatimid Caliphate expelled Christians from Jerusalem. In time, the Catholic Church gained political power. Pope Urban II sanctioned the move to take Jerusalem from the Fatimid. This began the first of several Crusades.[69] The Ottoman Empire would gain control and hold power until the end of WWI when the League of Nations administered the areas they formally controlled as well as those controlled by Germany.[70]

The Catholic Church established inquisitions to root out heresy.[71] While much of this was sectarian, in Spain and Rome these attacks were committed primarily on Jews and Muslims. Many fled Spain and Rome to avoid persecution. Others faced the choice of convert or die; hence the birth of the Marranos and Moriscos.[72][73] People were tortured, drowned, forced to do public penance and killed.

Millions were killed in the religious battles that culminated in the creation of Pakistan.[74]Coptic Christians have been singled out in the Middle East. Many have been killed in Egypt or displaced from Muslim majority countries.[75] Christian persecution in the Middle East has reached a point where even the *New York Times* wrote an article decrying "Is This the End of Christianity in the Middle East?"[76] Sectarian violence has also been common among sects in Christianity and Islam. The most obvious examples are the Thirty Years' War and the recent conflicts in Syria and Iraq.

Leaders with no religious affiliation can also be detrimental to religious freedom. Socialist countries like the USSR, Albania, and China banned all religious practices. "In China, churches were burned and open practice of religion was dangerous. The persecution reached its climax during the Cultural Revolution when all religion became a special target for Red Guard malevolence." [77] In contrast to banning religions, there are 43 countries with state-sanctioned religions today, diminishing the exercise of other religions.[78]

DICTATORS

Dictators occupy a special area of human depravity. They share a toxic combination of narcissism, violence, and lack of empathy. They use violence and intimidation to gain power, ramp it up to maintain power, and will use any scorched earth tactic, usually short of suicidal means, to kill as many on their way down. Stalin, Mao, Hitler, Pol Pot, Duvalier, Amin, Bokassa, Kim, and Assad, these names engender thoughts of the most abhorrent acts man has inflicted on others.

They killed indiscriminately, tortured their detractors, and sought greater power. Some raped, most stole, and they all wanted absolute adulation. In the case of Kim, Assad, and Duvalier, they passed the power on to their children. In addition to the constant brutality, they also limited freedom and sapped their respective countries of valuable resources. They made their citizens poorer and orchestrated the world's largest genocides.

CULTURE

Cannibalism was practiced in several cultures. African albinos butchered and ate humans to obtain magical powers. The Aztecs and Incans engaged in the practice as a sacrificial religious rite, as did the Iroquois, Mowak, and other Native American tribes. A cult in Australia and Papua New Guinea was found practicing cannibalism in 2012.[79]

Human sacrifice is another practice that was common in ancient history. Many polytheistic religions made these sacrifices to their gods. The Phoenicians and Carthaginians, the Shang and Zhou dynasties of China, native Hawaiians, and the Incans all practiced human sacrifice.[80] Some west Africans and Indians were still performing human sacrifices well into the 19th century. Sometimes these practices led to a clash with other cultures.

Here's an interesting exchange between the British colonists and Hindus addressing a cultural issue. The British colonists in India banned Sati, a religious funeral practice of burning widows alive on their husband's funeral pyre. When the Hindu priests complained, arguing it is their custom, Sir Chares Napier, Major General of the Bombay Army said, "Be it so. This burning of widows is your custom; prepare the funeral pile. But my nation has also a custom. When men burn women alive we hang them, and confiscate all their property. My carpenters shall therefore erect gibbets on which to hang all concerned when the widow is consumed. Let us all act according to national customs."[81]

SEXUAL DEPRAVITY

Some may not see sexual depravity as a human flaw. It is common in today's culture to say that people should be free to do what they want to do. Still others will say that as a civilized society, we *should* make distinctions between acceptable and unacceptable behavior. Homosexuality, fornication, and adultery are all but normative in modern society. The acts we're describing here are different.

Bestiality, rape, incest, pedophilia, and necrophilia are sexual acts that most find reprehensible. Not only do these acts take place, but they are not new to modern society. Pederasty was common in Greek society.[82] The Romans were notorious for their sexual exploits. The mere mention of Caligula elicits images of sexual excess. While these stories are re-told in a folksy manner, keep in mind that many of these acts were done, as they are today, without consent of the other party, unless you think a horse can sign a consent pledge. This separates these acts from those of consenting adults.

HUMAN EXPERIMENTATION

Inhumane medical testing is another example of human evil. Most were cloaked in military necessity or medical advances. The Tuskegee Institute lied to black patients and denied them treatment for Syphilis.[83] Nazis conducted several experiments on prisoners including 1,500 pairs of twins and artificially inseminating nearly 300 women.[84] Japan conducted barbaric chemical and biological research on humans in its Unit 731 top secret program.[85] USSR and North Korea intentionally poisoned people, while South Africa forced 900 people to have sexual reassignment surgery.[86] [87]Lastly, over 200 million women and girls throughout Africa, Asia, and the Middle East have been subjected to female genital mutilation according to the World Health Organization.

LEGAL INEQUALITY

In history, many have treated the minorities among them unfairly, but some implemented laws to keep them oppressed. The United States had Jim Crow laws, South Africa had Apartheid, and Australia had laws regulating its Aborigine population. Some minorities have only been given partial rights. The Ottoman Empire, for instance, allowed non-Muslims to practice their religions but they could not have full citizenship rights unless they converted. Today, India and Pakistan still have caste systems, and Russia, Iran, and many countries in Africa and Latin America have discriminatory LGBT laws. Legal inequality also exists for women, with over 150 countries that have laws limiting women's rights.

COMMUNISM

Most will probably disagree with the idea of communism being a human flaw. But think about it logically, we believe that treating people fairly is a moral good. Communism's expressed purpose is to treat one class of people better than another class of people. If we want equality, then treating groups differently should be frowned upon; whether it's oppression or preference. The dangers of communism are increased by the fact that it is cloaked in benevolence.

Their plan to help the poor is to take over the means of production so the revenue goes to the government rather than individuals. The proceeds are then used to provide for the people equally. They say this will result in a better quality of life. The problem with this plan is two-fold: (1) the government is not set up to run industries, and (2) the current owners are not willing to just walk away.

People go into business because they have an idea or a particular skill. They put in a lot of time and nurture their business like it's their baby. The government doesn't have the same industry knowledge or passion for the business. Also, if someone builds the business and is told to turn it over, they won't do it voluntarily. This will lead to oppression as the government will have to take the business by force. The same goes for all other property they want turned over to the government.

Take a look at current and past communist countries: China, USSR, Venezuela, Cambodia, Cuba, and Angola; did any of them lift people out of poverty? Of course not. They had, or continue to have, a few wealthy people and lots of poor people. The difference between communist countries and their capitalist counterparts is that their poor are poorer and the capitalist countries have a middle class.

This is why communist countries have more oppression. If you allow so much power to be concentrated within the government, it's natural that people will start to resist. In communism, the whole system is held together by control; without it, the system falls apart. It's also an 'all in' proposition. It cannot be successful if some of the people are practicing and some are not. Because of this, the government is obliged to oppress freedom. Some will say that the wealthy have too much power. This is true but they do not make the rules that govern us. They don't decide if you can own a gun or set tax levels. Any power they have is dwarfed by that of the government. They have to comply with government regulations while the government answers to no one.

UNITED STATES

Since most of the discussion throughout this book will be about the United States, it's important to highlight its history here. The US has committed many of the terrible acts listed above, this is not unique. When US history is viewed, however, it tends to be viewed more harshly than that of other countries. Much of the negativity is centered on slavery and its treatment of Native Americans. In addressing these issues, it's important to look at them in relation to the rest of the world at that time.

When discussing slavery, most people lay the blame at the feet of America. For my entire life, I've heard blacks say slavery existed in America for 400 years. They were wrong on both accounts; the length of enslavement and the simplicity of blaming America.

The transatlantic slave trade began in the 1480s, when Portugal first bought and kidnapped black Africans and took them to Europe where it was fashionable to have them as pages or servants. There is little account of slavery among African tribes being common. However, we do know that it became a lucrative business for them and most of northern and western Africa participated. Spain and Britain quickly joined Portugal in transporting slaves to the west, including its territories in North America and the Caribbean.

Before all of this, Arabs carried slaves from central Africa across the Sahara Desert. The Arab slave trade, the longest in history, lasted 1,300 years, more than three times as long as the Atlantic slave trade and began 700 years earlier.[88] It is important to note that when the slaves arrived in North America, there was no United States. For over 150 years, the slaves were in land occupied and controlled by Britain, France, and Spain.

The entire slave trade was controlled by the Portuguese, the Spanish, and the British. All of the slave ships were owned and operated by these three countries. When Britain ended the slave trade in 1807, the same year the US ended the practice, it continued in Brazil and Cuba for another 53 years. History books fail to point this out. They all say that the slaves were transported to 'America.' They may mean the continent, but the country is implied.

When told about this, most say it's a distinction without a difference. This is not consistent with conventional belief. When a country is controlled by a foreign power and the people rise up against it, that country is considered a new nation. For example, Mexico won its independence from Spain. When we look back on history, we don't say that Mexico controlled the slave trade or conquered the Aztecs, even though the land where it took place is now Mexico. If this is the case, why is there no distinction between Britain and America?

The bottom line is viewing slavery as solely an American problem is short-sighted and simplistic. In no way is this an effort to excuse the US. The point is that no one should be excused. Yet somehow, African tribes, Arab nations, Britain, Portugal, Native Americans, and Spain all get a pass. Take colonization, North America was controlled by five European nations: Britain, France, Portugal, Russia, and Spain. The biggest colonizers were Spain and Portugal, who controlled the early slave trade and all of Latin America. Spain also controlled Central America and the Gulf of Mexico, home to New Orleans. Take a look at the interesting way in which Spain was recently received.

In June of 2018, New Orleans celebrated its 300th anniversary. This, a city founded by French colonialists, ceded by them to the Spanish Empire, re-taken by the French under Napoleon and eventually sold to the US. At the celebration, New Orleans Mayor, LaToya Cantrell, presented King Felipe and Queen Letizia of Spain with the key to the city saying, "New Orleans would not be where it is without Spain."[89] To analyze Spain's treatment adequately, let's go to the logic board:

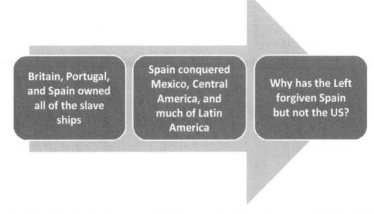

Again, Spain is honored, France is forgiven, and the US, the country that never held a colony, is left being viewed as the oppressor.

NATIVE AMERICANS

The pre-colonial accounts of Native Americans are difficult to express with any detail. The problem is two-fold: (1) there are many Native American tribes, and (2) we have no definitive evidence.

Because there were so many tribes, 567 recognized by the US government, they cannot all be viewed in the same way. There were many different languages, customs, and cultures. Some were aggressive; for them, warring was a way of life.[90] While others were more communal in nature. Because of this, their interactions with the Europeans were different. There were tribes the Europeans respected and some they viewed as savages, as referenced in the Declaration of Independence.

As far as evidence is concerned, all of the accounts are one-sided. Written evidence comes primarily from the Europeans giving us often exaggerated accounts of bloodthirsty natives attacking with impunity. Conversely, there is nothing written from the long period prior to colonization. What we get, therefore, is the account of the natives themselves. This, undoubtedly, is also a skewed view. This is how we get the common narrative that indigenous people were passively smoking peace pipes, enjoying life, then Columbus came and killed half of them; President Jackson sent the rest to reservations. This is an incomplete story. What can be surmised through archaeology indicates that the tribes did have conflicts. As Bamforth states,

"Intertribal warfare was intense throughout the Great Plains during the 1700s and 1800s, and archeological data indicate that warfare was present prior to this time. Human skeletons from as early as the Woodland Period (250 B.C. to A.D. 900) show occasional marks of violence, but conflict intensified during and after the thirteenth century, by which time farmers were well established in the Plains. After 1250, villages were often destroyed by fire, and human skeletons regularly show marks of violence, scalping, and other mutilations. Warfare was most intense along the Missouri River in the present-day Dakotas, where ancestors of the Mandans, Hidatsas, and Arikaras were at war with each other, and towns inhabited by as many as 1,000 people were often fortified with ditch and palisade defenses. Excavations at the Crow Creek site, an ancestral Arikara town dated to 1325, revealed the bodies of 486 people–men, women, and children, essentially the town's entire population–in a mass grave. These individuals had been scalped and dismembered, and their bones showed clear evidence of severe malnutrition, suggesting that violence resulted from competition for food, probably due to local overpopulation and climatic deterioration."[91]

So here we have evidence of warfare, genocide and violence. Then there are the cases of pillaging of settlers, horse stealing, and kidnapping of children.[92] This was a practice of just a few tribes and was mostly a response to tensions with settlers, but imagine your child being ripped from you. Or worse, being killed in front of your children and having them raised by your murderers.[93] Several tribes also participated in the enslavement of black Africans, as indicated in the section on slavery.

This doesn't negate the fact that the role of the US was devastating and morally corrupt. But the narrative that this was America's intent from its beginning is simply not true. In the Northwest Ordinance of 1787, article 3 states, "Religion, morality, and knowledge, being necessary to good government and the happiness of mankind, schools and the means of education shall forever be encouraged. The utmost good faith shall always be observed towards the Indians; their lands and property shall never be taken from them without their consent; and, in their property, rights, and liberty, they shall never be invaded or disturbed, unless in just and lawful wars authorized by Congress; but laws founded in justice and humanity, shall from time to time be made for preventing wrongs being done to them, and for preserving peace and friendship with them." [94]

Because the government's actions took a turn for the worse doesn't change the original intent. These terrible acts were due in equal parts to Native American raids, cultural differences, and American 'Manifest Destiny.' Many tribes did not have the same views on economy and property as the Europeans. For instance, they looked at the land as communal. One should take what he needs, without excess, but without borders. This view caused conflict with the settlers.

When the settlers found a desired piece of land, they took ownership of it. In their minds, there was no issue in doing so because no one owned a deed and the US government gave land for free as an incentive to encourage expansion.[95] For many Native Americans, the concept of land ownership didn't exist. If they wanted something on that land they were within their right to take it. This is where the cultural clash came into play. It was not a case of right or wrong, just different philosophies. It does beg the question, how is it so easy to say the Europeans stole land that the Native Americans didn't believe they owned?

The bottom line is that US history is no different from world history. The examples described above show that people have warred, attacked, subjugated, and otherwise harmed others for millennia. There are countless more instances, but the samples above were chosen to show that these acts were not limited to any specific, country, religion, or race of people.

Look at the Code of Hammurabi. These are Babylonian laws, from the 18th century BC, concerning: adultery, slavery, slander, theft, contract disputes, and more; 282 in all. Ignoring the specifics of the laws, their existence shows the human condition. These laws would not have been needed if our nature inclined us to do the right thing. Meaning, as far back as 3,700 years ago, 'civilized' societies were dealing with the same human flaws we deal with today.[96]

History illustrates two key realizations relating to equality: (1) You cannot police human nature, and (2) equality is impossible. Once you understand that the flaw of man is universal, you begin to appreciate the difficulty—no, impossibility—of policing it. In a fight for equality, you must discourage behavior that causes inequality and punish it when it happens. These laws exist. People do what they do because they think they can get away with it or they don't care. Murder is against the law, yet we have thousands of murders each year. One cannot regulate human nature.

The first problem causes the second one. In this politically charged climate, people debate which system of government is best, some prefer socialism, others prefer capitalism. The truth is, both would work fine if human nature wasn't flawed. Everyone would be equal and no one would show preference or desire more. In fact, you wouldn't need to have leaders to enforce the system. The inherent flaw of man makes this theoretical example impossible to implement.

Someone will always want more or be inclined to cheat. As long as this is a possibility, the sharing system cannot work. Think of the conquerors discussed earlier. Genghis Khan or Alexander the Great should have been complacent. They were wealthy leaders with lots of land and power (This, by the way is already unequal). Yet, they attacked other kingdoms to amass more. The kingdoms they defeated were not treated fairly. Conversely, the conquerors did not offer them an opportunity to be co-monarchs.

Knowing this, we should focus on what we can control. Instead, many believe that tinkering with the system will solve the problem. History shows us, from draconian enforcement of laws to anything goes, from monarchies to oligarchies, from capitalism to socialism, it's been tried in some form. In every circumstance one of the following took place: (1) it failed, (2) inequalities arose and people rebelled, (3) there was internal strife and the system was attacked, or (4) an external force conquered them. Capitalism isn't perfect, it's just the best of all of the systems we have.

Human nature is unchanging and eventually one of these things, or a variation of them, will put pressure on a society's way of life. This means there will be inequality in every society, even in a utopian one. Perfect is often the enemy of the good, and many of us spend too much time trying to fix everything rather than improve what we can.

Take the climate change crowd for example. They truly care about the planet and want to improve conditions, which can be a noble thing. However, making improvements is not the same as 'saving the planet.' The planet is millions of years old and has gone through an infinite amount of changes. Whatever your views on fossil fuels and other man-made causes of global warming may be, thinking that a few thousand people choosing not to have children or banning plastic straws in America is going to make a measurable impact is not just foolish, it shows an excessive level of self-importance.

The same logic can be applied to achieving equality. Man has committed millions of permutations of atrocities on other men, yet some believe they have the answer. As it says in Ecclesiastes 1:9, there is nothing new under the sun. I chronicled this brief summation of history in this chapter to show that they are being a bit presumptuous with their simplistic solutions and generous with their belief in the intrinsic good of mankind.

Finally, another advantage of looking at history is that it gives us context. Once we accept that people are not inherently good and those human flaws cut across all diversity categories: race, ethnicity, class, religion, national origin, and gender we can better assess how our system of government performs.

This is critically important as we will see in the next chapter. Some like to take the shining beacon on the hill and reduce it to an oppressive, racist nation. This is a blatant blurring of the truth. There have been missteps and atrocities along the way, which we will discuss. However, our forefathers knew they were not perfect. Their goal from the beginning was not perfection but to form 'a more perfect union.' In that respect, the achievements of America were greater than any other nation in history.

The problem with those who operate with the lack of context or understanding is that they try to judge every generation by their own and since they have knowledge and advancements that weren't available before and they think that they're superior to the others, they want to dismiss any good that was done because of prior bad acts.

This is how they can look back on 'uncivilized' societies and judge them for human sacrifice, nature gods, slavery and witch trials and think we've evolved. We are healthier, richer, and have better access to information. Yet, we have serial killers, suicides, sex trafficking, and drive-by shootings. This does not describe a more civilized society.

One of the best explanations of the flaws of judging past generations against one's own was given by the late, great Charles Krauthammer. He warned of looking back at the founding fathers and dismissing much of the great work they did because of the evils of slavery. He posited that one day, future generations will look at us as primitive for some reason we don't see; maybe being carnivores. He suggests there may come a time when one of the 20th century greats, say Einstein, may have his accomplishments dismissed because he ate meat.

For example, let's assume we passed laws banning the consumption of meat in 2020. By 2040, the entire meat industry has been dismantled, including any black-market sellers, and the average college student has never tasted meat. In just 50 years, former carnivores are comprised of only senior citizens. Fast forward to 2120, 100 years since the ban, and the shift will be complete.

If someone looked back and wanted to quote an economist like Thomas Sowell or Paul Krugman, people would discount them saying, "Who cares what they said, they ate animals!" Radio stations would no longer play greats like Sinatra, Led Zeppelin, and Beyoncé. Mobs would ban many books and demand that statues of MLK, Obama, Reagan, and Michael Brown come down. Much of society would view these people, and any other meat eaters, just one century from now, the same way many view the founding fathers today, over two hundred years later.

We abhor slavery, as we should, but we should not discount everything said in the Bible because at that time people owned slaves. This is not a wise way to judge. Keep this in mind, When God saw the wickedness of man and knew they would not turn away from it, He decided to destroy all of mankind. He said, "I will destroy man whom I have created from the face of the earth, both man, and beast, and the creeping thing, and the fowls of the air; for it repenteth me that I have made them." Noah, however, found favor in the eyes of the Lord because he was, "a just man and perfect *in his generation.*"[97]

· 2 ·

How the Fight Got Hijacked

The history of African-American repression in this country rose from government-sanctioned racism.

– Rand Paul

There were two primary objectives of the previous chapter. The first was to clearly establish that human nature is unchanging. The other was to show that those Americans who voraciously point out the many flaws of the US have a limited view of their country. They minimize the many accomplishments while highlighting the bad acts, or they don't acknowledge the ubiquity of those bad acts throughout the world. Because it may have appeared that I was defending America, detractors will say it was simply an attempt to excuse these bad acts. That changes here, as it is important to know the country's ugly past to understand why we ever had to fight for equality.

While America didn't create the practice of chattel slavery, which was much more brutal than indentured servitude or the conquering slavery of antiquity, many of the men who founded the country willfully participated in the practice inherited from their British predecessors. The practice was so engrained in the economy of the South that the country, sadly, could not find a diplomatic way to end it.

After the Civil War, we saw the creation of the Ku Klux Klan. Its primary mission was to suppress the rights of the former slaves and to overthrow the Republican government in the South. The situation was made worse by Lincoln picking Andrew Johnson, a Confederate-sympathizing Democrat, as his second vice president. Johnson would assume office after Lincoln's assassination. He did nothing to stop the reign of terror inflicted on blacks and granted members of the Confederacy full pardons.

Many of those former Confederates went back to their home states and assumed roles in local government. Some became judges and congressmen. This allowed them to establish the black codes and enact Jim Crow laws.[98] When the federal government did try to take action, it didn't always get assistance from the courts.

President Grant pushed to put a stop to the actions of the Klan. The Republicans in Congress passed enforcement acts and Grant suspended habeas corpus to aggressively attack the Klan. Though he was very effective, the Supreme Court, in *United States v. Cruikshank* (1876), ruled it was unconstitutional for the federal government to take jurisdiction of crimes that should be handled by the states. This after several white men were convicted in the Colfax massacre.[99]

Later, the Supreme Court upheld the constitutionality of racial segregation in *Plessy v. Ferguson* (1896). This decision led to the resurgence of the Klan. Because of this, lynching became increasingly common. While blacks were lynched by racist whites, without provocation, this gave rise to unfettered acts of vigilantism. By the time the practice was stamped out, over 4,000 people had been killed, more than one-third of whom were white. The numbers are unknown, but several Mexicans and Chinese were also lynched.[100]

Because of the ugly history of the South, many in the North look down on them. They consider themselves to be morally superior because the South fought to preserve this moral blight on our country. While this is true, it does not mean the North was a welcoming oasis for blacks. Slavery had been legal in all 13 British colonies prior to the Revolutionary War. It would be naïve to think that the racist views regarding blacks went away immediately when the northern states abolished slavery. It didn't happen in the South after the Civil War; why would the North be any different?

In the North, there was a strong contingent of abolitionists and a façade of freedom not available in the South. Unfortunately, what most former slaves found waiting for them in the Northern states was Jim Crow by another name. Blacks were either refused admission to, or segregated in, hotels, restaurants, and theaters. Most lived in poor, segregated neighborhoods.

What the government did with Jim Crow laws in the South, the citizens did in the North, and the government turned a blind eye to it. Businesses refused service to blacks. While the North didn't have laws banning blacks from living in certain neighborhoods, it was nearly impossible for successful blacks to find a home in predominately white areas. Finding employment was also difficult. Blacks were blocked from union-controlled jobs. Violence and intimidation were also factors in the North, just as they were in the South. The North had its share of racial killings and white riots.[101]

While no other group's mistreatment sank to the level of blacks, every other group faced some level of discrimination that needed to be addressed. Women were not just discriminated against, they were made invisible. Think of this, black men were once considered property, yet they got the right to vote fifty years before white women. Married women were totally beholden to their husbands. They could not own property or sign contracts. Women were discouraged from attending school, and many careers were closed to women.

Poor whites were also disenfranchised. Most worked as sharecroppers and did not own land, thus, owing to the prevalence of property requirements, they were not allowed to vote. They had no formal education and lived at the bottom of a de facto caste system. Leading up to the Civil War, many poor whites fought to maintain slavery, as they were told that freed slaves would take away their livelihood. After the war, those in power encouraged an 'us-versus-them' mentality as a way to maintain control. When blacks were granted citizenship, much of the South enacted poll taxes to block them from voting; this also kept poor whites from the polls for decades.

Most of the history of Native Americans has been reduced to the Trail of Tears, but their mistreatment continued long after. They suffered the difficulties and discrimination that most minority groups faced. However, the biggest sin Native Americans were subjected to is one that only black Americans can relate to; the theft of their culture. On the reservations, the native people were 'Americanized.' They were stripped of their tribal garb, forced to learn English, their hair was cut short, and they were introduced to Christianity. Many immigrant groups assimilated to make their lives easier, but none were forced by the government to do so.[102]

Native Americans also lived in limbo within the US. They were part of the US, but were not citizens. This created confusion as to when they were sovereign and when the federal government had a say. They had a form of tribal government, but they had to adhere to federal laws. They couldn't vote, but Native American veterans in WWII represented the largest percentage of any ethnic group. They were not fully made citizens of the U.S until 1924. Later, there would be a push to move them off the reservation and into the general society, causing them to lose even more land.

Immigrants had it hard throughout history in America. Those arguing for illegal immigration often say, "We are a nation of immigrants!" They wax nostalgic about the idyllic treatment immigrants received from the late 19th century through the end of WWII, but they leave out the not-so-glamorous true details.

Immigrants arriving by ship were separated by class, with the affluent getting preference. They were given physical and legal exams. This included a series of questions to determine background, intent, and to ensure they would not seek financial assistance. Based on this, people were admitted, interned, or immediately deported. Later there would be a series of laws that restricted naturalization, set quotas, created taxes, and limited immigration from certain countries.

Chinese immigrants came to take advantage of the gold rush and work the former plantations after slavery was abolished. They were attacked by settlers, forced into segregated neighborhoods, and subjected to the same housing and marriage restrictions as blacks. Many Chinese women were forced into prostitution, making the sex trade a lucrative business.

As for the men, they were integral in construction of the first Transcontinental Railroad, however, they were paid far less than their white counterparts and not given board or lodging as was the custom for whites. For instance, in 1850, during the gold rush, California enacted the Foreign Miners' Tax Act. It mandated that all non-citizens pay $20 per month, which was subsequently reduced to $3 per month. The idea was to reduce the number of Chinese and Mexicans working in the mines.

In Los Angeles in 1871, a mob of white men attacked and robbed Chinese immigrants, killing nearly two dozen. Justice was averted as the convictions of the few men charged were overturned.[103] This was followed by the Chinese Exclusion Act of 1882, which cut off the flow of Chinese immigrants to the US. In 1924, twenty-six years before *Brown v. Board of Education*, a Chinese-American girl was prohibited from attending a high school in Bolivar County, Mississippi (*Lum v. Rice*).[104]

Mistreatment of immigrants was not limited to racial minorities. Germans, Italians, Poles, and Slavs were all viewed as 'different.' Most were ostracized, living in slums. Most people are aware of the Japanese citizens who were interned during WWII but few know that During WWI, German immigrants were put in camps.[105] Like black Americans, immigrants were not considered for many jobs, leaving them competing with native-born blacks for low-wage jobs. Because blacks were paid less and didn't suffer from a language barrier, they were often hired first. This created animosity and an inevitable 'battle at the bottom.' Minorities, mostly blacks, were beaten and intimidated from keeping jobs, again with little recourse from the government.

While most immigrants came for opportunities, others were escaping tyranny. Even with this immediate threat, some were denied entry to the US. When several Jews seeking asylum were turned away from Cuba, President Roosevelt refused to allow them into the country, sending them back to the horrors of Germany. Despite this, many Nicaraguans, Cubans, and Armenians were given asylum. Jews were later also allowed entry. Unfortunately, selective acceptance was the norm. Since our government was anti-communist, fleeing a communist regime was better for you than fleeing an authoritarian regime, even if the treatment was equally bad.

Because of this, Guatemalans, Salvadorans, and Haitians were less likely to get asylum. For Cubans, it was easier to gain access fleeing Castro than it was if you were fleeing Batista. However, this was not always the case. After the fall of Saigon and the ascension of communism, Vietnamese and Cambodians sought refuge in America. California Governor Jerry Brown refused to give them asylum.[106]

The goal of the civil rights movement was to put to an end these 'separate but equal' laws and practices. It is important to note, however, that many blacks did not want to fully integrate with whites. The problem with separate but equal is that the separation was one way and there was nothing remotely resembling equality about it. White facilities were nicer, more abundant, and better stocked. Blacks had no equal alternatives to department stores, hotel chains, or restaurants.

Where they were allowed entry, they were treated poorly. Many places had separate entrances. In department stores, blacks had to guess what size to buy because they were not allowed to try on clothing. Once they bought the items, they could not return them to the store. Black entertainers were allowed to perform in white venues but couldn't eat in them, stay at the hotel, or enter the venues through the main entrance.

Separation even looked different. Blacks sat in the back of the bus. If there were no seats in the front, a white man could sit in the colored section, even if it meant a black passenger had to stand. While blacks could not sit at the lunch counter at Woolworth's, a white man had every right to go to the black owned restaurant or bar. If things in practice had been as the name stated, few would have complained. The point here is that the movement was about ending the practice of subjugation. It was never a full-throated plea for integration.

The country had reached a crossroad. It took nearly 100 years to go from the revolution that started a nation, one whose founders knew that slavery had to end but didn't believe they could end it and successfully achieve independence, to the war to end slavery and save the union. By the mid-1960s, the country was 100 years removed from the Civil War and nearing its bicentennial. Though significant progress had been made, we had yet to achieve the meaning of Jefferson's decree that "all men are created equal."

Since that time, we had held slaves, forced Native Americans onto reservations, enacted laws that suppressed freedom, interned Japanese citizens, and completely ignored women. After waiting hundreds of years for slavery to end and enduring another hundred years of intimidation, murders, and subjugation, blacks were not willing to wait another one hundred years for full equality. Something had to be done.

The passing of the Civil Rights Act of 1964 and the Voting Rights Act of 1965 was supposed to complete the journey. Jim Crow laws were repealed and protections were put in place to prevent discrimination against people on the basis of race, color, religion, sex, or national origin. But like with the 15th amendment, which gave blacks the right to vote, discrimination didn't stop; it just became covert.

People found creative ways to continue their discriminatory practices. Racism was not going to disappear overnight because of the passage of a couple laws. Blacks were still not welcomed in most of white society. Many employers simply went from posting signs telling blacks not to apply to accepting their applications and throwing them away. If pushed, they would interview some black candidates but find a reason not to hire them. This hindered the full effect of the law.

In addition to this, there was another obstacle to overcome; a skills gap. For many years, blacks were excluded from many jobs and industries. Even the public jobs were highly restrictive and often segregated. There were limited opportunities for blacks to learn trades or enter licensed careers like medicine and law. This would make it difficult for blacks to increase their status even with the new laws. Nixon took the first step to close that skills gap.

In 1969, President Nixon signed an executive order known as the Philadelphia Plan.[107] In it, he set goals for employment of blacks. This was a major change in approach. Before this, the goal was to remove the legal barriers to entry that were preventing blacks from attaining full access to all of America's opportunities. This executive order was saying, rightly so, that blacks had been at a disadvantage for so long and many were finding ways around the new laws protecting them, so 'affirmative action' needed to be taken.

Nixon's executive order was challenged but the court dismissed the challenge in *Contractors Association of Eastern Pennsylvania v. Secretary of Labor* (1971). This victory led to a series of Supreme Court cases that shifted the court into a gray area. Was their role affirming the constitutionality of laws or legislating the feelings and thoughts of the citizenry?

In *United Steelworkers of America v. Weber* (1979), a white employee sued, claiming he was passed over for a training program by less qualified minorities. The employer and union had agreed to make 50% of the positions available to blacks. Positions were filled by seniority within each racial group. The court held the practice constitutional for private parties "to eliminate traditional patterns of racial segregation." It was also intended to be temporary. The justices said there was no undue burden suffered by the plaintiff. I'm sure the employee who sued felt differently.

In *Fullilove v. Klutznick* (1980), the Supreme Court upheld a congressionally-enacted 10 percent minority business set-aside of federal funds for state and local public works. Here, the Court stressed the remedial nature of the set-aside. In *US v. Paradise* and *Johnson v. Santa Clara County Transportation Agency (1987)*, the Court upheld a promotion requirement that stated for every white candidate promoted, a qualified African American would also be promoted. This was basically a quota, which the courts contend is unconstitutional.

Lastly in *Johnson v. Transportation Agency* (1987), the Court upheld an employer's affirmative action plan that allowed gender to be considered as a positive factor when choosing among qualified candidates for jobs in which women were severely underrepresented.

What the courts, and Nixon's executive order, tried to do had the right intent but the wrong methodology. In Jim Crow laws, black codes, and poll taxes, we saw legislators pass unconstitutional laws based on their racist views and desire for an unequal outcome. The way you correct unconstitutional laws is to strike them down, not to pass equally unconstitutional laws. If the courts were wrong, as in Dred Scott, the decision can be challenged and a later court can overturn it.

In the black community, there has been an ongoing demand for reparations. In reality, from the late 1960s to the early 1980s, that's what we got, albeit unspecified, weak, and poorly executed. There were laws that stated that certain groups had fewer rights. The 1964 civil rights law said everyone must be treated the same. Legally, this was the equality everyone sought. It, however, didn't address how citizens treated each other or the huge deficit from which blacks and other minorities were starting. This is why affirmative action was implemented.

Affirmative action said that, though we are legally equal, there are built-in disadvantages for blacks and we need to create ways to give them assistance. What are reparations if not special treatment due to previous wrongs? The problem with affirmative action is they didn't specify the reason, didn't make the plans robust enough, and didn't set a clear scope or length.

Instead of affirmative action programs, the right move would have been reparations. My suggestion would have been to give blacks free tuition to state schools for one generation. To prepare them for college, resources would have been given to every public school with a black student population greater than 50%. For those not interested or prepared for college, skills training or free apprenticeships would have been provided. While this would not have addressed the racist problem, it would have gone a long way toward closing the skills gap.

The plan would also have a sunset date. The expectation would be that as blacks got more opportunities and started to rise, the vitriol against them would continue to subside. Eventually, things would progress to the point that ignoring civil rights laws would be the exception rather than the rule. If we hadn't reached that point, the plan could have been extended.

Look at the Chinese. They were racially profiled, violently attacked, and legally suppressed. They had the added challenges of a language barrier, yet, in spite of this treatment, they are among the most prosperous and successful groups in the country today. They have higher household incomes and lower poverty rates than that of whites. Later, we will discuss reasons for this. My point is, had the approach to assist blacks been done properly, we could be performing at the same level.

What we got, however, were open-ended programs that were, instead of black specific, aimed at 'minorities.' It's been nearly 50 years since Nixon's executive order, and these affirmative action programs, while still in effect, benefit other minority groups far more than blacks. Unless you're a straight white male, you're in a protected class today. Not addressing the unique animus towards blacks left them rightfully feeling that enough wasn't done. The majority of blacks faced open disregard for the newly implemented laws, and these actions were not nearly as broad as the discrimination. Allowing one or two companies to give a few blacks preference is not the same as giving the entire group the opportunity to advance.

In addition to creating weak programs, which is the primary reason blacks still demand reparations, there were constitutional problems to these actions. What the courts started to do was legislate from the bench rather than interpret the Constitution. You can't say that a law that discriminates against a person based on innate characteristics is wrong, then pass laws that give preferences on those same characteristics. Whatever your thoughts on affirmative action or these court decisions, you must acknowledge that this is not consistent with the goal of equality.

If gender can be considered as a positive factor, as in the Supreme Court case against the transportation agency, doesn't logic portend that considering it a negative factor should also be an option? If one employer can say 'having a woman in the role would be a plus', another should be able to say 'but I don't think a woman would be a good fit.' Allowing both of these takes would create a slippery slope, but only allowing one creates inequality.

The problem is that the civil rights laws had gone about as far as laws could go and maintain constitutionality. What we needed was less racism, not more laws. These moves towards preference were designed to force people to stop being racist. They were doomed to fail because you can't regulate feelings. If the government passes a law forcing landlords to rent to blacks, racists will just go from posting 'no blacks' signs to telling them there were no rooms available.

Even when steps are taken to help minorities, the results are usually mixed. In the case of minority government contracts, much of the work they're contracting out is highly specified. Since the past skills gap wasn't properly addressed, government officials find that there are not enough minority businesses that meet the minimum requirements. The white-owned firms are then given exemptions to contract the work to non-minorities. The results don't match the mandate.

Only the sentiments of the majority could change the acceptability of racist actions. Like John Rankin before them, whites who understood that discrimination was a morally repugnant aspect of our nation felt compelled to act. This was a great challenge and would take time but there were signs that the culture was changing.

In March of 1965, civil rights activists organized a march from Selma to Montgomery to register blacks to vote. After Jimmie Lee Jackson was killed by an Alabama state trooper, a group of protestors began to march to the capital. While crossing the Edmund Pettis Bridge, they were met by state troopers who attacked them with nightsticks and tear gas. Two days later, on March 9th, a crowd three times the size of the previous march, consisting of whites and blacks, approached the bridge again.

The whites who were present were motivated by the violent beatings from the first attempt, which was aired on TV.[108] This is but one example of whites having enough of the mistreatment of blacks. It would take a lot more action to overcome the seething resistance to black equality, but like the abolitionists before them, the moral understanding of right and wrong was there. Unfortunately, it may have taken decades for the motivation of whites to reach the level necessary to affect meaningful change.

In addition to continued racial injustices, there were social problems taking hold of the country. To mitigate them, the federal government began taking actions to help those suffering from a variety of these issues. For the first time in American history, the government was taking an active role in the lives of its citizens on a grand scale. Johnson's war on poverty, Nixon's affirmative action, Carter's Department of Education, and Reagan's war on drugs are all examples of the government moving in the direction of social engineering.

While much progress has obviously been made, these efforts did not create the benefits those who implemented them expected. All government actions, no matter how well-intentioned, have unintended consequences, and we were about to learn that they can lead to disastrous results.

Desegregation was important, but the law only prevented people from being denied access; it could not address white flight. If you look at many neighborhoods and public-school systems, they are still segregated. In some respects, it's worse. When blacks were not allowed to live in white neighborhoods, it forced middle-class blacks to live among working class and poorer blacks. Once this impediment was removed, more affluent blacks moved to other areas, making former mixed income black neighborhoods predominately poor black neighborhoods.

Many will say that this is systemic. It is true in some cases, but more often it's simple economics. Public schools are funded primarily by property taxes. When neighborhoods have mixed income residents and many businesses, schools tend to received adequate funding. When whites moved and affluent blacks followed, the schools were left to rely on revenue from homes with the lowest property values and renters. Without the support of the middle-class incomes, many businesses closed or moved. This had a devastating effect on the tax base. Unfortunately, there is no law we can implement to correct this.

President Johnson convened a group to determine the best way to implement his war on poverty. He appointed Daniel Patrick Moynihan, Assistant Secretary of Labor for Policy, Planning, and Research. His goal was to find the root causes to best attack the poverty issue. He was surprised by the results.

In 1965, Daniel Patrick Moynihan submitted his findings: *The Negro Family: The Case for National Action*. In it, he argued that the rise of single mothers in the black community was contributing to increased poverty rates and warned that if not properly addressed, it would lead to an impending crisis in the black community. He was quickly attacked. Women attacked him for overstating the need for male role models while many blacks chided him for blaming the victim. While he did say the problem resulted from a negative culture, he blamed those cultural problems on slavery and subsequent Jim Crow laws. In spite of his detailed research, few took heed.

It is clear that not only did his predictions come true, but the effects were far worse. At the time of the Moynihan Report, 24% of black infants and 3.1% of white infants were born to single mothers. The percentage for blacks has nearly tripled but the increase for whites has been nine-fold. Other groups are also high, with Native Americans at 66%, Hispanics at 53%, and Asians at 17%. In fact, the national percentage of 40.6 is 60% greater than the 1965 stat for blacks he thought was at a dangerous level.[109] Why is this a problem?

This was the beginning of a cultural shift. It was so subtle that few noticed it. While this was taking place, there was a generation of young people who were pushing back against traditional norms. The feminist movement and sexual revolution would slowly move our society away from structure or judgment of behavior. What Moynihan saw coming, primarily in the black community, was about to sweep the nation and would not be confined to parenting changes.

People were starting to marry less and have more children out of wedlock, mostly raised without a father. These single mothers would be more likely to turn to government welfare programs to make ends meet. This slowly chipped away at the pride and work ethic that was so prevalent in America. In one generation, many went from refusing handouts, even when they were blocked from many opportunities, to expecting government assistance. An entitlement mentality began to take hold.

As this continued, it was portrayed on TV and in movies which, in turn, was mirrored back into society. We went from TV shows with strong male patriarchs like *Father Knows Best* and *Make Room for Daddy*; to dad as buffoon in shows like *According to Jim* and *Married with Children*; to absent in *What's Happening* and *Mom*. For years there was a stigma attached to being a single mother. This faded, eventually leading to the rise of *Maury*, a television program that showcased women willing to confront multiple paramours to determine which was the father of her child; all for the world to see.

Many people had grown up poor and found a way to make a living. They were frugal and saved. They had to, there were no programs to fall back on. Over time, people started to spend more and save less, partially to keep up with their neighbors and partially to please their children. Parents went from trying to give their children the greatest opportunity to giving them whatever they wanted. They went from strict disciplinarians to friends.

For decades, the American dream had been to buy a house and save for the future. This grew into living lavishly. We collectively adopted Gordon Gecko's credo 'greed is good.' Middle-class families leveraged themselves to buy the biggest house or fanciest car. Poor people spent an unusually high percentage of their income on luxuries. It became common to see people waiting in line for days to buy Michael Jordan's latest sneakers.

We had officially reached a level of narcissism never before seen. Over the next couple of decades, people would put their careers before marriage and children and buy into the idea that you can have it all. Those who saw this shift coming dubbed it the 'Me Generation.' This created an environment conducive to demand preference. We had abandoned many of our principles, become selfish, and wanted to achieve without putting in the effort. If things didn't work out, it wasn't our fault. To make matters worse, we had also become less religious and more litigious.

All of this led us to our current state of self-absorption. Smart phones and social media have given us a world lacking conversation. Because of this, interaction, emotion, and connections are now manufactured. People post their entire lives on social media, hoping 'likes' will replace what we used to get from interpersonal relationships. Reality TV shows are everywhere; each upping the ante on bad behavior.

Now everyone wants to be famous. Worse, they don't even care what they're famous for. They've seen people become household names for riding a bicycle off of a roof, making a sex tape, hooking up with strangers, and being the worst contestant in a singing competition. Then there are the people we look at to make our lives seem better like the hoarders, 600-pound people, 'housewives' who show that money doesn't make you happy, and live police chases.

Only time will tell where we go from here. Hopefully, the pendulum hasn't swung too far. Much of this dramatic shift that's taken place over the last 50 years is due to social experimentation that got out of hand. We can't say for sure how much would be different without it, but the evidence is clear that government intervention along with the abandoning of traditional values accelerated the shift.

Being young as this was evolving, it took a while for me to understand that things were changing. At first, I ignored it. Then I thought it was odd but didn't see it as a larger problem. In the last ten years, things have gotten so extreme that it's hard to miss and none of us should ignore it. Now, I actively fight the negative cultural shift and speak out whenever possible. It's been twenty years, but I still remember the first time I truly noticed the shift. It was Tuesday, February 24, 1998.

My best friend and I were watching ESPN and the women's basketball game between UCONN and Villanova had just started. At the tip, a UCONN player controlled the ball and passed to Nykesha Sales who gingerly motioned toward the basket and scored an uncontested layup. A Villanova player was allowed to do the same on the other end. This, we later learned, was pre-arranged by the two coaches.

Sales was a star player for the UCONN team. In the second-to-last game of the season, she ruptured her right Achilles' tendon. Her season was over, and as a senior, so was her career at UCONN.

At the time of her injury, she was two points from breaking the all-time scoring record at UCONN, held by Kerry Bascom.[110]

UCONN coach Geno Auriemma, decided it would be a 'sign of gratitude' from the university for all that Sales had given the program. My friend said, "Wow, they just let Nykesha Sales break the UCONN scoring record!" to which I replied, "Did she really break it?" I felt something wasn't right, and for the first time, I said something. I went on, "Is this fair to the current title holder?"

Nothing about this is fair. I'm sure no one had ever stood aside while Bascom made a shot. And while Sales was far more talented than Bascom, doesn't that make Bascom's achievement all the more important? What about all the other talented players who didn't achieve everything they were capable of due to bad luck? It's unfair that Jim Kelly doesn't have a Super Bowl ring because some other guy missed a routinely made field goal 'wide right.' Can we just etch his name on a trophy?

When you give someone something and take from someone else, it's not equality. With another game and the tournament to follow, Sales would have easily broken the record had she stayed healthy; but she didn't stay healthy. Let's look back at Bascom's career. Maybe we'll find that she missed some games due to illness. Should we give her make-up games to increase her scoring total?

This is just one example, but from there I noticed it more. People say they want equality, but do not understand what they are complaining about is the lack of equal outcome, not equal opportunity. This desire to control the outcome of a situation generally starts with good intentions. Either a concern for someone's feelings or trying to right a perceived wrong.

Unfortunately, the very nature of this interference is aiding in the inequality one is trying to prevent.

Those with traditional values and those who fought simply to level the playing field are dinosaurs. Today they put qualifiers around demands. Instead of justice they demand 'social justice' and instead of the truth they openly tell 'my truth.' This new outcome-based equality makes it easy to justify any means to achieve their utopian goals.

Too many poor people? Tax the rich more. Not enough blacks enrolled at your college? Lower the standards. Someone loses a race? Give him a trophy. Responding to perceived injustices may feel good and give a façade of equality, but all it does is give a false sense of progress, to the detriment of innocent bystanders. Let's review the new move to minimize competition.

We used to think that competition was good and helped build character. We promoted teamwork, and taught children to be good winners and, better, good losers. It was supposed to give you a feeling of accomplishment when your hard work paid off; that has all changed.

First there was the move to give participation trophies. Giving people trophies for showing up minimized the accomplishments of the winners. Worse, once you take this step, it becomes easier to go further down this destructive path. Many schools implemented the mercy rule, stopping games when a team has what is considered an insurmountable lead. If it's done to prevent injury that would be fine, but in most cases, it's done to prevent hurt feelings. "Why should kids have to go through that humiliation?" some would ask. Wouldn't it be better to use the loss as a teachable moment? Also, it eliminates the opportunity for the winning coach to give his players who don't see much action a chance to play.

Next was the pitch to have kids play organized games and not keep score. There is no plausible reason to do this. The logical response to this is that kids will keep score in their heads anyway. If that's the case, we should just make it easy for them and put it on the scoreboard.

Ironically, professional sports seem to be the last bastion of merit-based equality. Athletes work hard to reach their goals and have to work to maintain their positions based solely on their own performance. In the NFL, a backup quarterback has to maintain his sharpness both to be ready in the event the starter is injured and to stay ahead of the third-string quarterback. Every year, starting quarterbacks are benched and replaced with their backups because their performance waned.

Surprisingly, the fans are in full support of this process. Even SJWs who spend their days demanding preference will plead with the coach of their favorite team to bench a failing quarterback, regardless of his race. In fact, it seems that all of the issues they protest for go out of the window in the goal of winning a championship.

There are no women in any of the major professional team sports. In addition, racial inequality is pervasive, income inequality is rampant and players walk around openly thanking God and praying in the end zone. Now some will point to Tim Tebow and the uproar his praying caused but that was more an attack on white Evangelicals as black players have been thanking God during games and in post-game interviews for years with not so much as a glance. Finally, count the number of openly gay or transgender players in the four major professional team sports. I would venture to say you can count them all on one hand and still be able to grip a baseball.

Professional sports even go against the 'everyone is a winner' mentality. In 2008, the NFL's Detroit Lions lost all 16 of their regular season games. It had to be tremendously embarrassing for them. It had been nearly 30 years since any team went winless and no team had lost 16 games before. Not one team eased up on them and none of the fans of the other teams supported letting them win. If the Lion players had been on the youth teams that protected their feelings, we can only imagine how they would have reacted to their record-setting season.

Focusing on merit seems to have worked quite well in sports. You would think the SJWs would be open to at least trying a merit-based approach in other arenas, but why replicate a proven method? Instead, diversity is paramount and nowhere is this contrast more drastic than in Hollywood. Hollywood is the biggest manipulator of culture. In television and movies, they use their platform to influence people on many hot button issues. This is deliberate and a major factor in the country's dramatic move to the left.

Wanting characters on TV to be more diverse feels like a good thing and having characters you identify with may be helpful. But trying to represent everyone is neither accurate nor a display of equality. Also, race and gender are not the only ways a person can identify with a character.

Take a cursory look at the casts of the most popular TV shows and you will find something that resembles a United Colors of Benetton ad more than a snapshot of society at-large. It seems like everyone has a minority friend, a gay neighbor or knows an immigrant fighting to stay in the country. Every family is interracial and they all have to deal with an evil capitalist.

The same goes for people in charge. Many on the left say we need more women and people of color in power. Turn on the TV and, viola, minorities have gotten instant promotions. I primarily watch procedural crime dramas or political shows. Take a look at the people in charge on these shows and you will notice an interesting trend:

Blacklist – Black FBI Director (one white male on a team of five)

Blindspot – Black FBI Director (one white male on a team of seven)

The Brave – Woman Deputy Director of the DIA (three white men on a team of eight)

Chicago Fire – Black Fire Chief

Chicago Med – Black woman Chief of Services in charge of the emergency room

Code Black – The head of the ER is a woman; the head nurse is a Hispanic male; the head of surgery is a black man

Criminal Minds – Woman in charge of BAU; boss is a woman (two white males on a team of seven)

Designated Survivor – Entire senior staff is minority; as are the head FBI and secret service agents

Law & Order SVU – Woman lieutenant (one white male on a team of five)

MacGyver – Female dwarf head of team (two white men on a team of six)

Madam Secretary – Female Secretary of State

SWAT – Black man in charge of team; Hispanic woman his boss

Taken – Black woman in charge of special extraction unit

Timeless – Hispanic, Lesbian woman in charge of team (one
white male on a team of six)

Every one of these shows has a diverse team and a minority in charge. This cannot be an accident. *Blue Bloods* and *Chicago PD* each have a white man but look closer. In the case of Blue Bloods, it is about a multi-generational family so it's pretty hard to create diversity in an Irish-Catholic, Boston family. However, the mayor, for most of the run, was a black man. He was replaced by a woman. On *Chicago PD*, all of the brass are black.

Don't get me wrong, I like seeing diversity on TV and think it's good to have minorities playing all types of roles. I was even one of those who nodded my head gleefully when I first saw minorities in roles rarely portrayed by blacks. But, one has to ask, what is the point of the diversity overkill? They argue equality. They say they simply want these roles to represent the actual makeup of the country. That is not what is represented above. This type of casting serves two purposes. Not only does it portray these positions from a utopian point of view; it also works as a way to diminish roles for white actors.

This is not a plea to assist white actors. It's only evidence that the arguments for equality on the left are disingenuous. No one believes that the next time a senior position at the FBI becomes vacant management is going to say, "I saw that black guy on *Blindspot* play the FBI director, maybe we should consider Tyrone for the role!"

The argument most often presented is not that it will influence the hiring manager in these situations, but that it will give minority children hope to believe they can reach these positions. This assumes the child is watching the TV in a vacuum. This 'hope' people are often talking about should come from the parents and others in their circle of influence. For instance, if a minority child wants to be a police chief after watching a TV show but the character is white, it is the parents' job to tell them there's nothing stopping them. Additionally, they can do an Internet search and find many minorities and women in these roles. The child is not limited to the actor hired to play the role.

Hollywood creates these situations in abundance to normalize them. If we see it enough, we are no longer shocked by it. Then when people argue against it, they seem extreme. This may be harmless when the issue is minority roles but it's far different when the situation is gay marriage, illegal immigration, violent crime, or religion. They portray gays in the best light, put illegals in the most compassionate of circumstances and create excuses for violent criminals. If done properly, it cannot help but influence the viewers' beliefs. It's pure propaganda.

This culture manipulation, done through a combination of entertainment and media coverage, is what shifted the public's view on same-sex marriage, drug enforcement, Christianity, and single parenthood. The change occurred virtually overnight. This is how Obama, Clinton, and others could say marriage was between a man and a woman yet, just a couple of years later, if you say it you're homophobic.

With the country collectively moving left, those with an agenda saw the perfect opportunity to increase their demands. In 1996,

Jesse Jackson led a boycott of the Academy Awards due to the lack of black nominees. In 2009 Kanye West interrupted the MTV Video Music Awards to say that Beyoncé deserved an award won by Taylor Swift and in 2017 Adele won the Grammy for album of the year. In her speech, she said, "… I can't possibly accept this award …" and gave her award to Beyoncé.[111]

These are telling because they are subjective awards. Unless they make the parameters ticket or album sales, you could never definitively say one person deserves an award over another. As for Jackson's protest, there are thousands of movies made every year and only five people are nominated in each acting category. If whites make the lion share of movies, it would seem the goal should be to focus on production not the academy. Another opportunity to address a root cause wasted.

These acts are now seeping into sports, where everything had been solely based on merit. In 2003, the NFL implemented the Rooney Rule, a policy that mandated minority candidates be interviewed for every head coaching and general manager vacancy. This seems like window dressing as the rule only stated that you interview them; there was nothing forcing you to hire anyone.

The biggest problem with the equality goals is that they focus on feelings and thoughts rather than actions. When you hear people call someone racist, sexist, homophobic, Islamophobic, or xenophobic, they are usually talking about something the person said or is perceived to believe. Even if they're right, we will never be able to regulate a person's thoughts; nor should we. Some will say this is important because it could determine the policies of a politician or the hiring practices of a manager. That is possible, but the evidence doesn't support it.

Lyndon Johnson was known for making racist remarks, but championed and signed the Civil Rights Act of 1964 into law.[112] President Truman is hailed for saving Israel though he made anti-Semitic comments.[113] Conversely, there are many politicians who say what people want to hear but implement policies that are as harmful as the comments the others expressed. They impose regressive taxes that disproportionately affect the poor and create situations that increase racial segregation.

In Chicago, for example, the politicians the SJWs voted for moved funds from predominately black neighborhoods to wealthier communities, upgraded train stations in more affluent neighborhoods before repairing stations or extending services to blighted areas in black communities, and they famously suppressed video of a questionable police shooting until after the election. These actions may be worse because they are done by the politicians who said what the SJWs wanted to hear. The politicians we perceived to be racist couldn't hurt us because we would never vote for them.

We have more laws, victim groups, and diversity programs than ever before. As a society, we are wildly diverse; multi-culturalism is the word of the day. There is plenty of diversity in pop culture and business. There are myriad black politicians as well as sheriffs and police chiefs, many of whom work in the south. All of this progress has been made yet we continue to have the same conversations about race.

Blacks are still segregated in many places in the country, have greater levels of poverty and health issues, and are incarcerated at greater percentages than any other group in America. There seems to be a problem with race that has continued in spite of civil rights legislation and affirmative action programs. Is the way to improve these conditions to continue the equality fight of the civil rights movement, or is there a better approach? We will now address the issue of racial equality.

· 3 ·

Racial Inequality

Dear Non-American Black, when you make the choice to come to America, you become black. Stop arguing. Stop saying I'm Jamaican or Ghanaian, America doesn't care.

– Chimamanda Ngozi Adichie

The goal of racial equality is flawed on its face and if your goal is flawed, achieving it is impossible. Blacks raise their children to look out for 'their own' and black intellectuals and celebrities say things like, "I'm rooting for everybody black."
[114] We are quick to acknowledge that people are tribal by nature, even self-segregating in many urban centers. Yet, we expect whites to be different. The essence of the SJWs definition of racial equality is: *blacks should focus on blacks and whites should focus on blacks.*

The chances that you can coerce whites to do this are nil. But even if you could create this dream world where whites decide to make everything equal, you'd still run into two problems: (1) the multi-culturalism of America, and (2) the true desires of those demanding equality.

In addressing the first problem, there are simply too many groups. While blacks actually mean black people when they say equality, most people are talking about inclusion and multi-culturalism. That means, equal representation of all groups: Hispanics, Asians, Native Americans, Muslims, et cetera, regardless of percentage of population. There's simply no way to achieve this and, even if there was a way, it would do nothing to address the concerns blacks are trying to remedy.

They demand more blacks on corporate boards, for example. If Starbucks has a 20-member board and we have equality based on population, there would be no more blacks on the board than there are now. You'd simply have a greater number from other minority groups. If the leadership board consisted of five members, they'd be in trouble.

The second and more troubling problem of racial equality is what the true demands are. Most who protest for greater equality don't want their words taken literally. They want more for the group they are representing. More blacks, for instance, doesn't mean equal to the percentage of the population. It means more than there are now and as many as we can get. You don't see them demanding fewer black players in the NBA and NFL even though that would be the necessary move to achieve equality. It's because if the inequality is in your favor, it's fine. This will never get us to the equality promised land.

Many on the left will bring up the obvious racism and subjugation of the past as a reason for the need to give deference to blacks in certain situations. While the history is clear; it also proves my point. The demand is to right wrongs, not to treat everyone the same. If that's your argument, own it. You must understand that what you are demanding is the opposite of equality. It's justifiable inequality. This, however, doesn't sound like something you could get the majority of people to sign up for.

It would be hard enough to convince whites to endorse equality of blacks to their own detriment, now you want them to voluntarily treat themselves less than others to equal out the past; a past, many will argue, they played no part in. This is not a game. You can't just give someone an uncontested layup. The same goes for preferences and set asides. Unless the outcome changes, there's no lasting effect. And you cannot force the outcomes, most realize that's a bridge too far.

The challenge with race relations, besides the fact that no one wants true equality, is that the way racism is expressed in society has changed, but those fighting it have not. During the civil rights movement, racism was easy to spot. There were laws barring specific groups from specific actions. There were signs everywhere. Today things are far different from that, yet racism is still alive.

While many believe there are still racist laws, these laws don't mention any specific group. This means that any racism perceived in the law is subjective. The wording is never racist, so one would have to look to the intent of the law. This is something that is nearly impossible to do. If they can't prove that the intent was racist, they should prove that the law does more harm than good, or propose a better one. Instead they just resort to marching and screaming, "Racist!"

They are shouting at ghosts. In the past, the racism was obvious, so all we had to do was bring attention to it. When whites hear racism now, they look around and they don't see anything. Blacks, in turn, constantly tell them that since they're white they'll never be able to see it; as if this is a good defense. They can't get the buy-in by saying, 'trust me, it's there.' Far too often, we use examples that aren't as clear cut as we believe them to be. We say the reason something happened is obviously racism when the reality is far less obvious. Let's look as some of these areas perceived to be racist, starting with the most obvious: the police.

POLICE

No other issue brings about a bigger debate on racism and its effects than policing. Whether it be the constitutionality of stop-and-frisk, or the national coverage of police shootings, the police have become the poster child, fairly or unfairly, of racism in America. We constantly hear from the Left that most of the police shootings are motivated by race. A more extreme version of this is the common refrain that the police are 'hunting down our young black men.' In order to deal with this complex problem and make a positive impact, one has to look at it objectively and use logic rather than emotion to determine causes and possible solutions.

Police obviously profile. We don't need a study to determine this. Even the most ardent police supporter cannot deny the alarming arrest and incarceration rates of blacks. This says nothing about whether they are guilty or not, but the police could not get that level or arrests without showing some heightened focus on a certain criminal profile or selected area.

The only thing we need to determine is whether or not the profiling is due to the officers' racist beliefs or something less nefarious. Police officers are trained to use their judgement to assess situations; accounting for environment, conditions, previous experience, and other factors to determine if they are potentially dangerous. Some profile solely based on their personal prejudices. The first is fine, the second is not. The challenge we face is how to know, in a given situation, if an officer's actions are due to operational expertise or racial bias.

People on the right often suggest that black on black crime is a far greater threat to the black community and accuse those who protest the police of ignoring it. When this accusation is leveled, the accusers are immediately rebuked for being insensitive and told that the situations are different and it's possible to address both issues. This argument is true, but to be fair, we don't address both, and saying that the situations are different is meaningless as it relates to improving either problem.

Here's an example that illustrates my point. Let's say you own a house and you have a door that is improperly sealed. Air is coming in and heat escapes. You also discover that your roof is leaking. Water is getting into the walls and you need buckets to capture the water on multiple floors. Both problems need to be fixed and have nothing to do with one another. This does not negate the fact that each will cost you money and you can't afford to fix both immediately. If you were to prioritize these repairs, not one person would choose the door. This is the real argument of black on black crime as it relates to police shootings.

Starting with Trayvon Martin, continuing to Michael Brown, and ramping up with the death of Freddie Gray, it has become the standard operating procedure of many blacks, with support from whites on the left, to take to the streets every time a black man is shot by a police officer, facts be damned. Conversely, shootings not involving police officers garner much less attention.

On June 17th, a week before the scheduled gay pride parade, Chicago's local ABC affiliate opened their broadcast with a five-minute segment on a historic event: Aurora, IL, celebrating its first gay pride parade. This was followed by weather and a shooting in the downtown area. Finally, they covered the weekend violence. The weekend shooting totals? 10 dead, 55 wounded. I guess 65 people being shot doesn't trump an inaugural gay pride parade. My point here is that when conservatives bring up black on black crime, they know it has nothing to do with police shootings; they are asking that you address the roof rather than the door.

If we want a true assessment, we must get beyond this 'cops are hunting us down' mentality. We have over one million officers nationwide who have dozens of interactions with the public every day, most without incident. This amounts to over one billion interactions per year. While life is precious and every police shooting needs to be investigated thoroughly, if the cops are hunting black men down, they're really bad at it.

However, looking at numbers independent of context is not enough. We hear that 987 people were killed by police in 2017 and an alarm goes off. But this number alone tells us nothing. When thinking of the billion interactions police collectively have with citizens, I don't think 987 people, while tragic, is an epidemic. However, what the headlines neglect to tell us is that of this total number, less than 70 were unarmed. This means that over 93% of the victims were carrying a weapon. I don't think these shootings should be considered when examining police brutality.

We also make the mistake of assuming that most of these people were just lying down, posing no threat. Some of the police involved shootings were during shootouts, while others are accompanied by video showing the suspect was the cause. This means that only in a small percentage of the already small number of shootings, is there evidence of potential wrongdoing on the part of the officer. More importantly, because it speaks to the claim of racial intent, only 17 of the 66 unarmed victims were black. This, unfortunately, goes unmentioned.

For some perspective, let's look at medical error. "A recent Johns Hopkins study found that medical errors are now the third leading cause of death in the US. Analyzing medical death rate data over an eight-year period, Johns Hopkins patient safety experts have calculated that more than 250,000 deaths per year are due to medical error in the US."[115] By contrast, police killings in the same time frame is roughly 7,000, or less than 3% of the deaths by medical error. Why are there no marches against hospitals and doctors? They endure more training, deal with more vulnerable people and encounter far fewer attacks than police officers do.

There are, however, many situations that don't involve a shooting. Harassment, unwarranted stops and overaggressive policing are also common complaints. These are complicated scenarios because it deals with basic human nature. They often boil down to the old adage, 'two wrongs don't make a right.' Say an officer notices a man he thinks is acting suspiciously and decides to engage. That man has done nothing wrong and is bothered by the unnecessary harassment. He addresses the officer rudely. The officer tenses up and there is an escalation of aggressive behavior on both sides. The officer was wrong in this case. He has been trained on how to proceed in these situations, but one cannot always suppress his nature. For the man who was questioned, he was technically right but didn't act in a manner that diffused the situation.

I know many people who will say it's wasn't the man's job to diffuse the situation. The officer is the one who should temper his emotions; the man had a right to be upset. I would agree except for one crucial thing; reality vs utopia. In an ideal situation, they would be right, but in an ideal situation the officer would not have approached the man. Reality says being right isn't always enough.

I liken it to a man waiting to cross the street. He waits for the walk sign, then proceeds. As he starts to walk, a car approaches. It looks as though it's going to speed through the light. The man clearly has the right of way. Should he continue to walk? If he does, and subsequently gets hit, he was clearly right. The driver, if caught, will likely go to jail. But is death or permanent damage worth proving a point?

In the previous scenario, the man was innocent. But contrary to the reports in the news, police do encounter criminals. These encounters make up much of the previous experience used in the first type of profiling we discussed. I am willing to give a little on police conduct, but I don't believe the SJWs will do the same when it comes to suspects. They act as if every person stopped by the police is innocent. Not only are they innocent of whatever conduct that may have lead up to their altercation with police, it's wrong to even mention their past.

Mention that Michael Brown had just stolen from a convenience store in Ferguson; it doesn't matter. Bring up Eric Garner's multiple arrests and felony conviction; you're deflecting. These things are important not only because all facts should be considered when conducting an investigation, but also because cops don't just appear from nowhere. In the overwhelming majority of these cases, they were called. Contrary to the image the Left paints of white officers driving around looking for blacks and hanging out of their windows shooting at them, they were there because someone called them for that specific situation, usually a local citizen or business owner.

When John Crawford III was shot in Walmart, the 911 operator told the officers he had a gun; when Quintonio LaGrier was shot in his home, his father had called 911 saying his life was being threatened; and when Laquan McDonald was shot 16 times by a Chicago cop, he had been vandalizing cars and slashed an officer's tires when confronted.[116] In all of these cases, and many of the other high-profile police shootings, the narrative portrayed in the press simply doesn't hold water.

Telling an officer that a violent crime is in progress, changes the manner in which he will approach the suspect. Note what the officers encountered when they arrived on the scene in each of the above cases. LaGrier wouldn't put down the bat, McDonald was walking in the middle of the street carrying a knife, and Crawford was holding a rifle (a toy but they didn't know it at the time). Even Eric Garner told the officers, "It stops today!" and "Don't touch me." Most people with negative opinions of police officers believe racial bias is the explanation for all of the problems. No one wants to look at the stats. That is until Harvard economics professor Roland G. Fryer, Jr. did an empirical analysis of racial differences in police use of force; with surprising results.[117]

His comprehensive study examined over 1,300 shootings spanning 15 years in 10 cities. It took into account the age of the suspect, the race of both the suspect and officers on scene, the time of day, the reason for the interaction, and several other factors. What Mr. Fryer found was that, "In shootings in these 10 cities involving officers, officers were more likely to fire their weapons without having first been attacked when the suspects were white." His study didn't stop there.

He went on to examine situations where the officers had sufficient reason to use lethal force but did not. He determined this by looking at arrest reports and examining where suspects shot at the officers, resisted arrest or tried to physically attack the officers. "Mr. Fryer found that in such situations, officers in Houston were about 20 percent less likely to shoot if the suspects were black."

The marchers and protesters all claim that police officers killing unarmed black men is an epidemic, this despite all evidence showing that claim is a fallacy. You can look at an individual shooting and determine that officer was wrong, but even if every shooting was wrong, it still wouldn't make the case for an epidemic. In the 16 years of Mr. Fryer's study, 1.6 million total arrests were made and officers fired their weapons only 507 times. This is consistent all over the country. Yet emotion takes over, so the protests continue.

Fryer did find that blacks were more susceptible to other forms of force from police officers. While officers were less likely to shoot a black suspect, they were 18% more likely, on average, to push a black suspect against the wall, throw him to the ground, pull a gun or use other forms of non-lethal force. He suggests this may be because there is a cost associated to shooting someone, but no cost for using non-lethal force. This may be true, but is only speculative, as the study doesn't provide any evidence. Fear of repercussions is definitely a factor. That is what's behind the so-called 'Ferguson Effect.'[118] I would argue that there is an additional cause for this behavior.

As difficult as it is to get blacks to take an objective look at police behavior and arrest stats, it's exponentially more difficult to get them to be introspective. Police have a huge stake in the direction a stop will take, but the person being stopped also has some responsibility. Yet many blacks refuse to see that their own actions contribute to the officer's escalation as well as the existence of racial profiling.

If a disproportionate amount of crimes are committed by blacks and much of the crime in a given city happens in predominately black neighborhoods, how can we expect cops to do that job for 10 or 20 years and not develop a profile? Perhaps we need to come to terms with the fact that store clerks don't follow us around because we're black, they follow us around because the last ten people who stole from them were black males between the ages of 13–20. Refusing to take a look at our own actions does our community a disservice and exacerbates the problem.

It is illogical to believe that Muslim Americans, the group that owns many of the stores in black neighborhoods, leave the suburbs to open stores in black neighborhoods because they hate blacks. The same goes for white cops 'policing' blacks. Most officers are assigned to a given area and would prefer to avoid confrontation. Many would prefer to work in safer neighborhoods, while others volunteer to work in the most dangerous neighborhoods because they want to give back and they think keeping the innocent people in those neighborhoods safe, the vast majority of the residents, is the honorable thing to do.

Whatever your view of police, I believe focusing on them as the problem in the black community is too broad and lacks focus. The police, in most cases, are simply enforcing laws. If you want to focus on police action, perhaps it would be better to address areas where their power is too great. For instance, in a free society, why should the police be able to stop you for any reason?

They have so much leeway for traffic stops, for example. I don't believe you can train the racist out of someone, but allowing officers to stop people for almost any reason affords a racist cop the opportunity to stop any black driver. You have to follow a lawful command given by an officer. Refusing to do so puts you and the officer in danger. Perhaps we should force our legislators to stop police from focusing on small infractions like seatbelt violations. Minimizing the interactions law abiding citizens have with law enforcement would help, but without the small infractions, municipalities would lose much needed revenue.

There are things we can do to make the system better but there is no magic fix, and equality won't work. Unless there is an equal distribution of crimes committed, there will never be equality in incarceration numbers or how certain segments of the population are perceived. Perception is reality, and blacks are going to have to change their reality to change the perception.

Even if you were able to make the necessary changes to improve race relations, it wouldn't happen. With the call going out to 'resist,' most people comply. It's easier to complain and post memes on social media than it is to do the real work. Many are not willing to civilly engage those in leadership positions if they disagree with them. When they do speak up, it's not about the things I mentioned.

If we had the same number of people talking about respecting authority, learning a trade, conflict resolution, the impact of absent fathers, and the role of God in our lives as we do the history of slavery, old white men, reparations, and the percentage of blacks at a given company, things could be different. But as it stands blacks are more concerned about placing blame than they are about finding solutions.

There are some issues that truly work to the detriment of blacks. Some were specifically designed to do so while others are the result of unintended consequences. Either way, challenging them is important and would be beneficial for society. But how do they play into the fight for equality and what is being done to rectify them? I'd like to take a look at three issues commonly viewed as targeting blacks: Redlining, drug sentencing and mandatory minimums.

REDLINING

Redlining is a practice specifically designed to use a geographic area, which generally represents a particular minority group, to deny that group services. This was primarily used to prevent blacks from getting mortgage loans. Otherwise qualified applicants were turned down for loans simply because they lived within the targeted area. While housing discrimination had been going on for years, Roosevelt's Federal Housing Authority created structured standards for the practice. For the next 30 years, it continued to be the method banks used to make lending decisions. In 1968, the Fair Housing Act was passed; it made redlining illegal, but it continued in different forms.

Many black customers were given higher interest rates than they deserved. In other cases, whites were cajoled into selling their property under its market value using fear tactics, only to sell those same homes to blacks at inflated prices. A form of these practices we still see going on today is intentionally limiting services to certain communities. We've often heard how hard it is to get a cab in certain areas. The same is true for other services. The term 'food desert' was coined to describe areas in the inner city where there is a lack of grocery stores and fresh produce.

My wife and I have had many situations where we needed repairs on our home. We called companies to get estimates only to have them tell us they do not service our area. This, in spite of the fact that we live in the city of Chicago and their business was also in the city. They weren't even subtle about it. In several cases, the companies put a list of zip codes they service on their website. Ours was often left off the list.

The solution to this problem is not as easy as it may seem. Redlining has been against the law for nearly 50 years, yet many claim it's still going on. It's difficult to believe that with government regulations, university surveys, social media, and many minority employees, a major institution would still be able to get away with those practices without anyone noticing. Two recent studies argue they found evidence of lenders using the practice, one by Reveal from the Center for Investigative Reporting, and the other by the local Fair Housing Center for Rights & Research in Cleveland. Their examples show obvious disparities but lack evidence of a racist origin. Here is what they found.

In the Philadelphia study, whites received 10 times as many conventional loans as blacks even though they represent a similar share of the population. In the article supporting the study, they illustrated the argument with the example of a woman who was turned down though she had a good credit score and made $60,000 per year. She was told her income wasn't consistent enough so she got a full-time job 'managing a million-dollar grant'. When this didn't work, she later found that an unpaid $284 electric bill tanked her credit score. Finally, she got the loan; when her partner, who is half white and half Japanese signed onto her application. This, in spite of the fact that her partner was a part-time grocery store employee whose bi-weekly income was $144.65.[119] This screams of racism, right?

There are a lot of assumptions used to make this point. It is safe to assume that of the 31 million records the researchers went through, they picked one of the stronger examples to make their point. If this is the case, their argument is pretty weak. The initial claim was that Ms. Faroul had a good credit score. If this is true, a $284 electric bill should not have 'tanked' it. Next, they listed her salary while downplaying the fact that it was a contract position. If she had a short work history and no permanent job, the salary wouldn't make much difference. A fair report would have also listed the loan amount she was attempting to get. Perhaps it was greater than her $60,000 salary could afford.

When she found full-time work, they listed her duties instead of her salary. One could infer that it was less than her $60,000 contract salary. Finally, they implied that someone who makes 72 dollars a week can easily get a mortgage if they are white. This ignores the fact that she 'signed onto' Faroul's loan, meaning *both* incomes were considered. Perhaps Franz's higher credit and a second person to go after in case of default was the reason the loan got approved. Not a strong case.

The second study reviewing Cleveland's Cuyahoga County made similar assumptions. Look at the data they compiled on application denials by race:

HOWARD HANNA MORTGAGE SERVICES	FIRST FEDERAL OF LAKEWOOD
Percent of applications denied in white tracts: 2.1%	Percent of applications denied in white tracts: 4.6%
Percent of applications denied in nonwhite tracts: 4.2%	Percent of applications denied in nonwhite tracts: 9.5%
CROSSCOUNTRY MORTGAGE INC.	**QUICKEN LOANS**
Percent of applications denied in white tracts: 4.7%	Percent of applications denied in white tracts: 19.8%
Percent of applications denied in nonwhite tracts: 8.7%	Percent of applications denied in nonwhite tracts: 29.8%
FIFTH THIRD MORTGAGE COMPANY	**PNC BANK**
Percent of applications denied in white tracts: 11.5%	Percent of applications denied in white tracts: 16.9%
Percent of applications denied in nonwhite tracts: 28.9%	Percent of applications denied in nonwhite tracts: 32.8%
THE HUNTINGTON NATIONAL BANK	**WELLS FARGO BANK**
Percent of applications denied in white tracts: 15.3%	Percent of applications denied in white tracts: 15.9%
Percent of applications denied in nonwhite tracts: 27.1%	Percent of applications denied in nonwhite tracts: 25.2%
THIRD FEDERAL SAVINGS & LOAN	**JPMORGAN CHASE BANK**
Percent of applications denied in white tracts: 5.9%	Percent of applications denied in white tracts: 20.7%
Percent of applications denied in nonwhite tracts: 17.5%	Percent of applications denied in nonwhite tracts: 30.0%

Their own findings show that these percentages vary largely by institution. It also shows that as the percentage of denials go up for nonwhites, it also goes up for whites. This shows that some banks simply make it harder to get a loan. While every bank did have higher denials for non-whites, this doesn't portend racist intent. On average, whites have higher incomes, better credit, and hold more wealth than minority groups. This could be the reason for the discrepancy in denials.[120]

If the assumption of the studies is right and the reason for the difference *is* racism, how do we combat it? For companies in industries deemed a public service, you could force them to serve the area. Taxi cabs, for instance, in most places are compelled to pick up anyone requesting a ride and take them to every neighborhood, but they are not forced to drive through every neighborhood looking for a fare. Should they be? If the population density is less and lower income people are less likely to hail a cab, should the company be forced to divert cabs to the areas anyway, at the possible loss of fares in more popular areas?

Ride-sharing came along to create new opportunities in the space. They definitely create more riding options for customer, but since they are a private company, they are not forced to drive in a particular area. If they offer rides in underserved areas it's because they notice the taxi companies missing an opportunity. This is a free market solution.

In some situations, it's more of a 'chicken or the egg' scenario. Are the costs greater because of the race or income of the residents or because of the known statistics of the area? Should an insurance company, for instance, be able to charge more for coverage in a low-income area because crime stats show there is a greater risk of burglary or theft, even if we believe the crime levels are a result of past racist practices? Further, we are no longer a free society if the government can force a company, Whole Foods for instance, to open a grocery store in a low-income neighborhood. This is where the fight for equality runs into a problem.

Often, I hear people say that in order to help those less fortunate, others are going to have to give up something. I completely agree; however, it's the compulsory action that I am opposed to. If companies or individuals are willing to sacrifice for the greater good, I applaud them. Forcing them removes the charitable act and is not an effective means to solve any problem. Even if we could convince legislators to do this, many businesses would eventually shut their doors. Either they would lose money, or feel it's not worth the additional risk. This scenario has repeated itself in black communities for decades.

DRUG SENTENCING

The debate, for many, as it relates to drug enforcement begins long before sentencing disparities. They wonder why, in a free society, we are trying to regulate behavior. Even those who disagree and believe drugs are bad and should be regulated or banned must admit that criminalizing it hasn't worked. We've spent billions on this so-called 'war on drugs' and nothing has improved. But as long as these drug offenses are illegal, we have to address the way sentencing is implemented.

The issue with drug sentencing has largely been the disparity between crack and powdered cocaine. The penalties are more severe for crack possession than powder, even with lesser amounts. Those opposed to these sentencing guidelines argue that they are racist, as those found in possession of crack are far more likely to be black. While these statistics cannot be disputed, it is not easy to determine the reasoning behind the legislation.

In the late eighties and early nineties, the demand for crack cocaine soared. It was deemed an epidemic by many in minority communities. Due to its low price, a greater number of people were able to obtain crack. While some argue it is not, as often promulgated, more addictive than powdered cocaine, the low cost allowed people to buy greater quantities, more often. This created more addicts and introduced the drug to an alarming number of children.

These skewed sentencing guidelines were born out of a real concern for the citizens or, as is often the case with government, unintended consequences. Many of the local politicians, most of whom were black, supported, even pushed these guidelines. It's easy to say they were wrong; most of them will admit that now.

What isn't so easy is concluding that the intent was to lock up black men.

MANDATORY MINIMUMS

Tied to the drug sentencing problem is that of mandatory minimums. Here is another area in which I agree with those arguing of its unfair nature. I will assume that the argument was to correct the problem of dangerous criminals getting sentences too light for their crimes. If this was happening, it sounds like there was a problem with the judicial appointments, not sentencing guidelines. Mandatory minimums take away discretion and context. Here is an example of what mandatory minimums can do.

In August of 2010, Marissa Alexander was attacked in her home by her estranged husband with whom she had an order of protection. She fired warning shots to get him to leave and was charged with aggravated assault with a deadly weapon. Her lawyer argued she was protected by the state's "Stand Your Ground" law, but the judge denied her claim. She was subsequently sentenced to 20 years in prison.[121] While it's true that she turned down a plea deal of three years, any logical person can see that sentencing her to 20 years is not justice.

It also doesn't address the biggest problem within the justice system: plea bargaining. Our constitution affords every citizen a right to a speedy trial; however, in most cases, defendants don't get a trial at all. It starts off innocently enough. The prosecutors don't want to spend the time and money to take every case to trial. Actually, with all of the people arrested, they simply don't have the manpower to do so. The result of this practice is unfair to the accused and hurts society in the long run.

Here's what often plays out in many cases across America. A person is arrested and is in possession of trace amounts of an illegal drug that would typically not lead to an arrest, but he is also in possession of an illegal weapon. When the prosecutor gets the case, he starts the plea-bargaining process. The suspect is offered reduced jail time and no felony if he pleads guilty to the drug charge. In turn, the gun charge is dropped. Now, the prosecutor has a quick win and the suspect gets less jail time; a win-win, right? Not really.

On the one hand, if there were problems with the stop or circumstances surrounding the arrest, they won't be brought to light. Most of the offenders don't have the best representation because of limited resources, so they are pleading to cases of which they may have been acquitted. Society is hurt because, if guilty, we have a possible violent offender officially charged with a misdemeanor drug charge. They will be let back out on the street and, due to the specifics of their conviction, not handled in the same manner a person with a felony gun charge would have been. While people claim they want to put an end to gun crimes, this is going on unchallenged.

Here is a specific case. My wife and I were robbed at gunpoint outside our home a few years ago. The man was captured and we were given a court date. The prosecutor offered him a plea deal but he turned it down. What we found is that in many of these cases, the victims don't show up to testify, so the suspects are advised to wait it out. If the victims don't show, they beat the case. Once he was informed we were there, he accepted the plea. We did not have to testify but stayed in court to observe the sentencing. To our surprise, the judge rejected the plea. Apparently, he had two similar prior offenses, both plea-bargained by the prosecutor. Treating these offenders as non-violent sets a dangerous precedent.

It's important to note that all of the negative effects of the criminal justice system are placed at the feet of the Republicans. This does not mesh with reality. The narrative is that racist Republicans introduced these laws to keep blacks in line. They decry Nixon and Reagan's war on drugs and law and order stances as code words for blacks. What they don't realize is where these so-called racist laws came from.

Former President Clinton is often blamed for the 'three-strikes' rule, but the Democrats' actions go far deeper than that. The bill was written by Joe Biden and sponsored in the house by Joe Brooks (D-TX). Of the 195 'no' votes, 131 were Republicans. [122] Additionally, both the Anti-Drug Abuse Acts of 1986 and 1988, which created mandatory minimums and criminalized crack cocaine more harshly than powder cocaine, were introduced by Democrats, James C. Wright, Jr. (D-TX)[123] and Thomas Foley (D-WA) respectively.[124]

Looking back even further, on March 25, 1971, the Congressional Black Caucus had a closed-door meeting with President Nixon. They demanded that he take more action to stop the flow of narcotics into urban neighborhoods. Nixon secretly recorded the session. Lastly in 1976, California Governor Jerry Brown signed into law new mandatory minimums widely believed to be the first step to the prison overcrowding problems the state would later see prior to Brown's resurgence as governor. [125] Somehow, all of this got blamed on Nixon and Reagan.

These policies may or may not be racist in intent but blacks are disproportionately affected. The problem is that in many cases there are other plausible explanations for the action taken. 50 years ago, it didn't matter if you were innocent or not, if you were black, you could be in danger. In today's scenarios, more often than not, the potential victim broke a law or had some deficiency that made the actions justifiable.

The racial equality fight does not reside with blacks alone. Today, millions of illegals, many from Mexico and Latin America, argue that they are being treated unfairly. They've been emboldened by Barack Obama who said he wanted to secure the border but secretly passed out flyers in Mexico promising SNAP benefits for illegals.[126] Later, he unilaterally created the Deferred Action for Childhood Arrivals (DACA), a mechanism for some to remain in the country legally. There is a process to change immigration laws and Obama's actions circumvented it.

Now, those here illegally march and protest, demanding citizenship. The unwavering support the Left gives illegal aliens is mind-boggling. This is not to say that I think it is right or feasible to deport millions of people. But what they're doing is compounding the problem.

With marching orders from the radicals, leftist politicians are openly defying federal law and pushing municipal and state legislation to promote illegal immigration. They rushed to make jurisdictions they control 'sanctuaries.' Next was the push to give illegals driver's licenses and now the right to vote in municipal elections.

In California, they recently named a school after Jose Antonio Vargas, a journalist who 'bravely' admitted being illegal.[127] They also appointed the first illegal to a government post.[128] In New York, Cesar Vargas was the first illegal immigrant to receive a license to practice law.[129] If Democrats are actively abetting illegal actions and, in some cases, putting the needs of illegals ahead of citizens, how can anyone take a fight against illegal immigration seriously? I also wonder, with illegal immigrants getting so much coverage, what happens to those who follow the law and wait? Where is their advocacy group?

As usual, the Left is oversimplifying the problem and only focusing on emotion. Recently, there has been an emotional debate about children being taken from their parents at the border when caught crossing at an area other than an established checkpoint. This situation needs to be dealt with soon, but the Left is losing sight of the reality of the situation. We all acknowledge that coming to America, illegally, is a tough decision to make. Most of the irrational people are only looking at one end of the problem and not the other.

If you think about what a parent has to go through to make that choice, it's heart-wrenching; worse if the child is being sent alone. This is what the Left is missing. Consider a tough decision you have to make; a new job, buying a house. You would create a list of pros and cons and weigh each one to make the best decision. These are poor people who have to pay a lot of money, risk crossing into multiple countries, avoid the Mexican cartels (if that's not who they're paying), assume a high probability of being raped (for young women), hope the coyote lives up to his end of the deal, pray they don't get caught, try to prevent their kid from being trafficked, all in varying temperatures with limited food and water.

The point here is that a parent would have considered all of these dire possibilities when deciding to take the journey or send their kids to the US. Being detained at the border is simply part of the process. It's a risk, but that risk is palatable when compared to the gamble of staying in their home country. That fact exemplifies just how bad the conditions are in many Latin American countries. Yet the Left believes ICE is the problem.

Racism will always be with us, as will every other type of human evil. We should not tolerate it, nor should we give it power. In order to make any progress towards racial equality, we have to start with what we can all agree on, then rationally go on from there. We'd lose the Left right from the start. They say they want to have an 'honest conversation about race,' then they proceed with dishonesty. One of their initial arguments is that blacks cannot be racist. Rationale is already gone.

Look at the way many blacks speak. They say the same things white racists say. Remember the math principle that states that if A=B then B=A? This applies to racism as well. White supremacists believe they are superior to blacks. They say things like, "The negro is inferior to the white man." No one would attempt to say that this is not inherently racist.

On the other hand, many blacks blame all the ills of the world on the white man. They say, "Whites are evil." In that statement they are not saying they are superior, in fact, they are normal; whites are just bad. By saying whites are evil, bad, conniving, violent, and dishonest, one can only deduce that they are inferior to the black man, who is normal. I call this the symmetric property of racism.

Many will say that blacks cannot be racist because of their lack of power. There are so many flaws to this argument. First, as is often the case with the Left, they redefined the word. There is no respected dictionary which has the caveat of power in its definition for racism. But for the sake of the argument, let's give it to them. Are they saying no black person has power? This shows a low opinion of blacks' success.

No one could say that Barack Obama doesn't have power, can he be racist? Ok, he's a unique case. How about Oprah Winfrey or LeBron James? Every celebrity, athlete or business man with a sizable fortune has power. Their words and actions influence millions. More importantly, they have a staff. They maintain several homes, have attorneys on retainer, have foundations, restaurants, clothing lines, etc., they definitely have enough power to be racists. It is not only the rich who can wield power. If a black man takes a white family hostage at gunpoint he, at least temporarily, has power. If the sole purpose of his action was his hatred for whites, I think we can conclude he is a racist.

In addition to the list of celebrities, politicians, and business people with power, there are all of the black people walking around screaming Black Power. How can you say you don't have enough power to be racist when you're constantly telling people about all the power you have? The truth is that most of them don't believe they have any power at all. They believe they are powerless so they tell themselves and everyone around them they have power in hopes of convincing themselves.

Lastly, the leaders of most African countries are black, do they have power? I believe if you ask white South Africans, they'd say yes. In March of this year, a proposal to amend Section 25 of the constitution allowing expropriation of land without any financial recompense passed in the South African parliament with a vote of 241 to 83.[130] This comes after the new president, Cyril Ramaphosa, said during his inauguration the he would speed up the transfer of land from white to black owners.[131] It seems that black Americans are the only group in world history genetically void of this human trait. Obviously, this is ridiculous.

They go on to argue that personal accountability is not a factor in how blacks are treated and anything they perceive as racist, even if race is not mentioned, is, in fact, proof of racism. They seem to be more concerned with perception than reality. Because they see racism everywhere, it's difficult to focus on one problem. Even when they can narrow it down, their message gets lost.

Black Lives Matter was founded to address what they deemed as systematic violence against blacks. They initially focused on police brutality and murders. As they grew, they got caught up in the culture of inclusivity. On their website, BLM lists its guiding principles. These principles include: Diversity, Queer and Transgender Affirming, Globalism, Empathy and Loving Engagement. If reversing years of mass incarceration and police violence is the goal, how is affirming transgender people and focusing on diversity going to advance this cause?

It seems like these activist and misguided politicians are bound to repeat the mistakes of presidents Nixon and Johnson. Any workable solution would have to be specific and comprehensive. We have groups who are prepared to discuss flaws within the system and others who are prepared to discuss flaws within the black community but few who will address both.

The lack of personal responsibility, poor education, disproportionate single-parent households, a job skills gap, and increasing government dependency has as much to do with the state of Black America as racism does. Anywhere there is racial inequality we should fight it, but unless we're willing to address all of the causes, we will be stuck in a perpetual ineffective civil rights movement.

· 4 ·

Income Inequality

Hip hip hooray, unemployment is down. What
does that mean to me in my life?

— Nancy Pelosi

While race is obviously the most emotionally charged and important of all of the inequality categories, income is the most talked about and the most universal. It makes sense. Regardless of your race, gender, sexual orientation, or religion, no one is exempt from economic risks. It is also the most subjective of all of the inequality concerns. The best way to address it is to determine if it is a problem that has reached a crisis point and to decide what role the government should play in solving the problem.

When looking at income statistics, everything is relative. In the US, people argue that the median income is not a fair wage, but most of the world lives on a fraction of that income. If you mention this as an example, you will likely hear that it is unfair to compare the US to other countries, this is the epitome of hypocrisy.

The Left is always suggesting that the US operate more like other countries. We need to impose Switzerland's healthcare system, Australia's gun control policies, and the Netherland's price reforms. Venezuela was often touted as an exemplar of what

America should be, prior to its recent collapse. The approach the Left routinely takes when judging the US is to point out the negative and ignore the good.

The problem with this is that it creates an illusion that we are in a desperate state. This is far from reality. Even if we concede that the US lags behind the countries mentioned above in some areas, the reality is more nuanced than they make it out to be. It does not mean that we lag behind these countries overall.

Take murder for instance. Homicide in America is a problem and needs to be addressed, but if you believed the mainstream media, we are the murder capital of the world. They constantly run stories stating, "Among developed nations, the US is far and away the most homicidal." They openly wonder why we're so much worse than the rest of the world. But the actual stats tell a different story. In 2017, the US was the 38th most violent country and of the 50 cities with the most homicides in the world, only Baltimore, New Orleans, and Detroit made the list, with none in the top 20.[132] With the dramatic increase of violent crime in Germany, Sweden, and the United Kingdom (London surpassed NYC for the first time), we may be falling further on that list. This illustrates that the US is far from the death trap those on the left make it out to be.

A clearer analysis, like the one above, can be done in every area, but when one takes the stance that things are bad, only data which supports that belief will be considered. This is how the Left approaches income disparities. One has to be capable of pointing out areas of improvement while still acknowledging that our poor live far better than the poor in most of the world.

In any conversation about income equality, the discussion should also include those with the greatest need. We have a large number of chronically unemployed and homeless people in the US. For such a rich nation, this should be a major concern. Most will agree that we have an obligation to help those in need. The difficulty lies in two areas: how we determine the threshold for need, and who renders the help.

The Left is confused about how this is addressed from a conservative point of view. It is often said that conservatives don't care about the poor or are unwilling to help others. They offer as proof the Republicans' call for welfare reform. Cutting social welfare programs that help the poor would make it more difficult for them to survive, they argue. They fail to realize that the objection to these programs is the rampant fraud and the fact that they do not work.

Even if operating as intended, these social programs are largely ineffective as they focus primarily on survival. This gives those in need little assistance and does nothing to help their future. Conservatives want the focus to be on independence. They want to move people from their current position to a higher economic bracket. The programs, as they currently operate, do nothing to encourage this. In some ways, people are incentivized to remain stagnant.

The number of people who receive help is also limited. These programs have eligibility requirements. No matter what formula is used to determine this, there will always be people left out who could use assistance. Also, people have situations arise that are out of their control, like a sudden decrease in hours, a medical emergency, or job loss. There needs to be a place for people to go to get short term assistance or services tailored to their specific needs.

Once it's determined what help is needed, the next step is to decide who administers it. This is where the differences are magnified. Progressives want the help to come from the government. They believe there should be a government safety net for everyone who needs it. Conservatives also believe the government should help, but it should be the last resort, not the first stop.

There should be fluid levels of assistance that people go to when in need. It should always start with family. They are the people closest to you with the greatest vested interest in your well-being. Of the people living in Section 8 housing or collecting welfare benefits, there has to be a sizable percentage with family who could give them aide. Why should the government subsidize a single mother and her child when she has a successful sibling nearby living alone in a two-bedroom apartment?

If there is no family around or they are unable or unwilling to assist, the person in need should try the greater community. They should seek assistance from extended family, friends, neighbors, church parishioners, and other members of the neighborhood. This is how much of the world gets by and how America supported the poor for over 200 years.

The next level of assistance should be organized charities. Shelters, soup kitchens, church programs, and other area organizations should be consulted. America is the most charitable country the world has ever known. We give billions to countless charities and when disaster strikes, here or abroad, we dig deeper. This spirit of charity is different in America, but most of us take it for granted.

We've all seen the turmoil Venezuela is going through. The economy has collapsed, the streets are dangers, and medical assistance is abysmal. Fabiola Zerpa has been writing articles about what he sees day-to-day in Venezuela. In an article about how bartering has become the new form of business transactions now that the currency has failed, he made an interesting observation, "Charity is also something new. I didn't grow up with the traditions of canned-food drives and volunteerism that are common in the US."[133]

This type of thinking is deemed evil on the left. They believe those in need are entitled to assistance and many Americans who struggle with poverty are increasingly subject to feel the same way. Religious adherents on the left strangely resist this approach as well. They say that, as believers, we have an obligation to help. I, and most conservatives, agree completely. This is why we donate so much. I contend that they are confused about who the Word is saying should give aide to the poor.

When the government gives aide, this has nothing to do with our obligation to give. We pay taxes and the government does as it pleases. We do not get the blame or credit for how they spend those funds. Our charity must be by choice. When America gives humanitarian aid to a foreign country, the citizens don't get to claim a percentage as charitable giving. The same goes for the Bible's calls to help the poor. We are to help, independent of government deeds.

It also takes a great level of hubris to proclaim you will defeat poverty. Everyone agrees that those in need deserve our compassion and assistance, but the social engineers on the left think they can end poverty. To the Christians on the left I ask, when Jesus said 'The poor you will always have with you' do you think he was wrong?

The bottom line is that assistance should flow from family to community to charities. Only after all of these have been exhausted and assistance is still needed should one go to the government for assistance. People underestimate the importance of non-governmental help. While I take issue with the lack of competence and speed in which the government administers its assistance, there is a much bigger problem.

Earlier, we discussed people falling through the cracks because they don't meet government eligibility requirements. For many, assistance at this crucial point could be the difference between holding on and falling into despair. The current system forces them to fall into despair in order to receive assistance. This assistance, in most cases, will not be commensurate with what they will need if they are allowed to fall that low. At this point, they will have a much more difficult time getting back to where they were.

For example, take a family of three with a household income of $75,000, above the national average. They own a home, a car, and have a child in daycare. Let's say they experience a job loss and the household income drops to $40,000. Few can absorb a 47% drop in income. They would try to cut out extras, but at such a drastic decrease, they will miss payments. Late notices will hurt their credit rating and some of the funds they saved by cutting back will go to the cost of finding a job. Most of us would agree that it is important to help this family before they lose their house or car rather than after they hit rock bottom. Government assistance for a family of this size carries a maximum income of around $27,000. They would not qualify. Fortunately, there are no guidelines for help from family and community and few from charities.

As with most things, good intentions have gotten in the way. The most effective approach would never be considered because it doesn't play well to the crowd guided by emotion. Instead of sporadic help that exacerbates the problem, the government should deal with crisis management and move on. Some have tried, but most fail because they only address one side of the problem.

Seattle has an increasing homelessness problem and the local politicians came up with a plan to combat it. In May of 2018, the Seattle City Council unanimously passed a 'head tax.' This tax will implement a $275 per employee fee, a compromise from the proposed $500, on businesses with gross revenues greater than $20 million per year. The funds are slated to build affordable housing and emergency homeless services.[134] The plan has a math problem.

Say, for instance, a company with $20 million in revenues and 2,000 employees has $2 million in EBITDA (Earnings Before Interest, Taxes, Depreciation, and Amortization). This is not rare, as many industries have an average profit margin that is less than 10%. The head tax for this company would be $550,000. In this case, the company would pay nearly 30% of its profit in additional taxes. This also makes it punitive to hire more employees.

No responsible businessman would pay this without making operational changes. Whether it's cutting staff to save money, passing the costs on to the consumer through increased prices or, in extreme cases, moving out of the city or closing the business; businesses will adjust. As with so many other government programs, the head tax will leave a host of negative unintended consequences in its wake.

In addition to being unfair, this plan does nothing to address the root causes of the problem. This is common, the Left throws money at a problem and walks away. A Chicago alderman has another seemingly unproductive plan. Ameya Pawar has proposed a universal basic income program. It would provide 1,000 families with a $500 monthly stipend—no strings attached.[135]

Pawar's plan is silly. Giving people money with no strings attached will hurt more than help. However, I am not opposed to government funded homeless shelters or other assistance for the indigent. The problem with Seattle's plan is the implementation of an unfair new tax and the lack of a detailed plan for the money's use. You may be wondering where I would get the funds to assist the homeless population without increasing taxes.

The proper way to do this is to take the funds from existing appropriations. We'd start by cutting other forms of welfare. There's nothing immoral about putting the needy behind the destitute. Homelessness is a human rights problem, a health problem, a sanitation problem and a moral problem. It's like triage, you help those with the most immediate need first.

This is not to say we should ignore those who fall through the cracks. There will no doubt be some who are not in dire need yet or are struggling and don't have family or friends to help. In these situations, the government can still offer assistance but in a far more 'hands off' way. In most of these cases, it involves a temporary situation like job loss or a medical bill. The person needs money for a few weeks or months to get by. Why not offer low interest loans with limited backing from the government? Obviously, some may default on the loans. But many would pay the loans back, drastically reducing the net amount spent on assistance. More importantly, it would encourage work ethic. The current system leads people to believe they are entitled. When you foster that belief, it calcifies.

When the social security act was enacted in 1936, eligibility began at the age of 65. However, the average life expectancy for men was 59. Life expectancy for women was 65 but most women were not eligible, nor were blacks. It's obvious that people were never intended to receive benefits. The few who did make it to 65 were expected to die after a few months. It wasn't retirement; it was insurance. Now people count on it to live out their days.

Selfishness affects the approach to these programs. If a politician suggests raising the retirement age, he risks being voted out of office. Whenever Congress adds a work requirement to receiving welfare benefits, they are met with opposition. Forcing someone to work for their benefits is cruel, some say. They even changed the terminology from welfare to entitlement. This is why loans are good. It doesn't just state that the money is to be paid back, it eliminates any belief that you're entitled to it.

Up to now, the discussion has been about the homeless and those in need of assistance. While those are major problems that need unique solutions, most of the SJWs would say that their fight is against income inequality. To that end, let's take a look at income inequality and see how, like every other argument they make, their logic is flawed, they're ignoring the obvious or they're lying to advance an agenda that's destined to fail.

One method they use to achieve equality is a minimum wage hike. For nearly a decade the Fight for 15 group has been advocating a $15 minimum wage. They have organized protests, many of which have been directed at fast-food and retail giants,

McDonald's and Wal-Mart. They are making a mistake pretending that every employer is as large as McDonald's and Wal-Mart, but they also show that they don't understand how businesses work.

Let's examine McDonald's. Let assume starting pay of $8 per hour with most making between $8 and $10 per hour their first year. They then have hourly supervisor positions that pay between $12 and $15 per hour; assistant managers who make around $35,000 and store managers who make $60,000. Now, if the starting pay went to $15 tomorrow, they'd have to pay employees who have experience more than entry-level employees, it is only fair. Let's give them $17. Now they make more than their supervisors so they'd be in line for a raise to say, $20. That's an annual salary of nearly $42,000. Assistant managers, in turn, would go to $50,000 and store managers $65,000.

When you tell the SJWs few businesses can absorb these enormous costs, they just shrug and say, "They have the money." This shouldn't determine if it's right to raise wages, but it is most likely untrue. Here's a quick explanation of profits to benefit the SJWs.

Many businesses operate with thin margins. Those in the service industry, industries more likely to employ low-skilled workers, rank among the lowest profit margins. The average profit margin for a grocery store, for example, is 2.5%. Restaurants and retail profits vary widely, generally 10–25%, based on whether they are high-end or value brands. Let's look at Wal-Mart, since McDonald's has so much tied up in real estate and the added complication of franchise revenue.

Wal-Mart has a profit margin of 8%, not a lot of money relative to their revenue. $15 an hour is a 61% increase for the average employee.[136] If we did the same for Wal-Mart as we did in the above McDonald's example, the additional labor costs would be 134% of their total profit.

Regardless of size, no business could afford giving their entire staff a raise all at once. Many would shut their doors. Those who don't close, will drastically raise their prices. This is what happens when you set wages based on employee needs rather than what the employer can pay.

The Left's biggest argument isn't about the level of any individual salaries. It is their belief that the gap between the wealthiest individuals and those at the bottom of the economic wrung is unfair. They lament the fact that some have billions while others work for low hourly wages. I call this the 3E syndrome. It is a bad combination of envy, emotion, and poor understanding of economics. They like to say that capitalism only helps the 1%. This is not true, but even if it were, capitalists should reply, socialism helps 0%. Which is better?

First, they act as if there is a finite amount of money. This argument implies that in order for Jeff Bezos to be the richest man in the world, someone else has to give up something. There is no logical basis for this. I liken their beliefs on income to President Trump's view on international trade deficits. Trump is correct in addressing countries, particularly China, who don't hold up their end of trade agreements. Currency manipulation and theft of intellectual property are serious offenses and he is right to attack. But it's his concern over the imbalance of trade that is no different than the Left's concern for income inequality.

This dangerous deficit he speaks of simply means we import more than we export. This fact is neutral. Whether it's bad or good depends upon many variables, but it is not bad on its face. Some things are imported because we cannot make them locally, take diamonds for instance. Other items are imported because a given country is the leading producer and therefore has expertise that creates added value, think Swiss watches. Finally, many items are imported because they are cheaper to import than to make.

Much of this is due to fewer regulations and far lower incomes in those countries. As much as we love 'American made' campaigns, many like the lower priced items. For many, the ability to buy items at lower prices is how they survive. When Trump adds a tariff to a particular product, it does nothing for the trade deficit. We still import more than we export. The only difference is those imports will cost consumers more money and the exports will cost more in other countries. As long as there are greater demands for their products than ours, there will be a deficit. The same logic can be used in the income debate.

A common practice of the SJWs when discussing statistics, is to take a number and use it as evidence of their argument, even when the number is out of context and doesn't make their point. One example of this is their constant reference to CEO salaries as they relate to the company's average worker. We can thank the Dodd-Frank leftist reform for this. While this makes the CEO look bad and out of touch, it has nothing to do with worker pay or income inequality.

Obviously, they're trying to say that if the CEO didn't get millions, the employees could make more money. Let's look at Wal-Mart again. Their CEO, Doug McMillon, has a total compensation of $22.8 million. According to *CNN Money*, that is 1,188 times the average worker's salary of $19,177.[137] This is clear evidence of greed in corporate America, right? Unfortunately, this word problem is missing one number. If we add the number of Wal-Mart employees to the equation, 2.3 million, we find that Doug could refuse his salary and divide it amongst the employees and they would each get a one-time payment of $9.91. Not exactly life changing money.

This is why you have to remove emotion from the equation and look at labor as a product. With this in mind, everything has a value. A salary is simply the value the customer, the employer in this case, puts on the product he's purchasing. That value is determined by many factors: skill level, difficulty of work, added value, education, etc.

Just as a customer in a retail store will look at several coffee makers and determine which machine to buy based on price, size, functionality, brand recognition, and many other factors, so too will an employer use several factors to determine who to hire and consequently what to pay them. In both cases, no third party should determine how that decision is made. That's why the *New York Times* had it right when they said the right minimum wage is $0.00.[138] This was obviously not today's *New York Times*.

This would also allow people to take less to prove themselves, lowering the barrier to entry for worker with no experience, formerly incarcerated individuals, and those facing various forms of discrimination. The fight for $15 will cause unintended consequences if accepted. Disabled workers will be hurt by drastic minimum wage increases because most employers, faced with the mandate to pay all workers the same, would opt to keep the most productive employees, the same logic holds for teens in poor neighborhoods.[139]

Raising wages arbitrarily or by government fiat will help very few. Let's go to the Logic Board for an example:

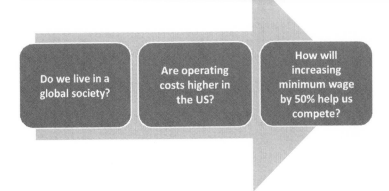

We exist in a global economy and are competing across borders. If two businesses operate in the same industry, one in America and one in a foreign country, our business climate will be a major factor in the difficulties the American company faces. If barriers to entry are greater, licensing and regulation processes are more difficult, labor is vastly higher, and the tax burden is greater, the American company is at a disadvantage. If you agree with the first two questions, you must explain how an across-the-board increase in labor costs will help American companies compete. Setting aside any quality differences, if the US company charges $129 for its finished product and the foreign country charges $79, why would anyone buy the product from the US company?

This isn't just a fairytale that could never happen. It's been going on for years. When companies laid off call center workers, they did not cease to have a call center. They just moved the operations to India. Call centers were the first to go, but computer programming, IT, virtual assistants, and medical transcription are quickly following. Everyone knows when manufacturing jobs went away that the products did not. Seems like we're looking to solve a big problem by creating a bigger one.

Another argument is that people should make the same salary for the same work. No logical person actually believes this. Here's a basic example. LeBron James made $33,285,709 for the 2017/2018 NBA season as a forward for the Cleveland Cavaliers. Larry Nancy Jr. made $1,471,382. They played the same position on the same team. It is safe to assume that they both had to go to the same practices, team meetings and other obligatory events. On game day, they both had to be at the stadium at the same time and were on the court during the entire game, yet no one believes Larry deserved what LeBron made. The same can be said for every other workplace.

Some people have more experience or more technical skills but they do the same job. They may have the same experience and education but one does a better job than the other or works harder. An employer has to be able to compensate his employees as he deems fit, even if he is occasionally unfair. There is no doubt that some employers will undervalue an employee either because of race, gender, previous salary, or just because they are cheap. As hard as this is for the SJWs to comprehend, this is ok. When faced with this situation, a potential employee should do one of three things:

A) Do not take the job. Hold out for a better opportunity

B) Take the job, prove your worth and petition for a raise

C) Take the job but continue to search for a better one

Employers who purposefully underpay their employees will suffer. Their good employees will be snatched up by their competitors. They will be left with employees who don't like their jobs and don't care about the product or service they provide. This will inevitably hurt their business. The only way this doesn't work is if every employer in a given industry underpays their employees and virtually colludes with one another. This is highly unlikely but if it happened, the employee could just leave that industry.

Another unintended consequence of raising the minimum wage would be the artificial inflation of the dollar. With the dollar worth less, you'd need more money to buy the same amount of stuff as before. In the end, people would have more money but would be in the same financial situation. Simply put, they'd get a 50% raise but the consumer price index would increase 50-55%; all smoke and mirrors. Some will point to past minimum wage hikes and say we didn't see this effect then, but we've never had 25% increases before or annual increases over multiple years. What we're talking about here is going from $7-10 per hour to $15 in a couple of years.

Recently, there has been a cry for a 'livable wage.' Bernie Sanders and others have even resurrected the call for a universal basic income. As well-meaning as these ideas are, each has a glaring flaw its proponents have yet to find a way around. Livable wage is simply a talking point. No one knows what that is. Everyone doesn't *need* the same wage to live. Using this logic, single people would get paid less than married people; a woman with one child less than one with three. This is no way to set wages and would be contrary to their other demand that everyone deserves the same pay.

I like the universal basic income plan. It's a great way to prove that it won't work and call the Left's bluff. The problem is the Left would implement it without making any other changes. My plan would be different. Let's give everyone a salary, no exclusions. I'd propose calculating the average each state pays out per recipient in government assistance and giving that amount, plus a 20% increase, to each resident. The payments would be made in monthly installments. Here's the rub, I would then eliminate every government assistance program and those over the poverty line would pay an increased amount back in taxes.

This will do two things: force people to be responsible for their own funds, and save money in the long run by eliminating fraud and the bloated administration costs associated with these programs. Here's how it would work.

If the average family in Illinois get $30,000 a year in TANF, food stamps, and housing assistance, I'd give them $36,000. A family in New York that receives $50,000 would get $60,000. Just think they'd get more money and they wouldn't have to go to that pesky office and fill out all of that paperwork. All you need to do is file taxes. All income up to that amount would be tax free. Everyone over a certain income level would pay the tax rate for that income but would also be assessed the annual state payment, basically giving it all back. That's the beauty, no qualifications, so no fraud, and no administration fees.

The Left would never go for it because they have to protect public sector jobs. Tens of thousands of people would be out of work at HHS, HUD and the IRS. The SJWs would love it, initially. They would soon notice, however, that when people didn't manage the money properly, they would have no government outlet for assistance. It seems just giving people money wouldn't solve the problems after all.

The true crisis in America is not income inequality; it is the diminishing work ethic and lack of marketable job skills. This is due to generational shifts that started with the baby boomers. Their parents had seen one, if not two, world wars and the Great Depression. They wanted to make life easier on their kids and were a bit too lax. The baby boomers grew up with free love and free choice. When they got older and had kids, they went one of two ways. They either overcorrected and were really strict parents or they tried to make up for the things they hadn't done and focused on work or school, leaving my generation to be raised by the TV, creating latchkey kids.

We, in turn, did what our grandparents did: gave our kids everything. Now they're teenagers and they've never had to lift a finger. We feel we're successful, so we should enjoy some conveniences, but those conveniences are stripping our children of character. We have cleaning people, landscapers, and dry cleaners. Children don't learn to cook, clean, or do laundry. You don't just wake up with a strong work ethic, and many parents don't or can't teach this to their children. Their mistakes will become our problems.

I began managing restaurants at a young age. I was just shy of 21 and most of my crew were older than me. I had to learn how to get the work done and gain their respect. My biggest lesson was that you have to be firm but fair. I tried bribing or negotiating but quickly realized it led to them always trying to get something from me.

Fast forward about twelve years and now I'm managing teens and people in their early twenties. It should have been easier. I was experienced and older. There should have been a level of respect built in that I had to earn before. Nothing could be further from the truth. When I told them to do something, they resisted or asked why I didn't get someone else to do it.

The marketable skill shortage is a side effect of the college crisis. We all want what's best for our children and that, so it seems, is a college education. A college-educated child is what owning a home used to be: a status of success. It has been commonly believed for years that a college education is not only the single greatest indicator of economic success, but those without one are doomed to entry-level jobs and minimum wage pay. This is no longer thought to be the case.

Because everyone is being groomed for college, no one learns specific skills. They literally call the program at most high schools, college prep. They are no longer teaching children how to learn and reason. Get them into college; that is the sole goal of high school now. We removed woodworking, shop, and home economics from high school, then totally ignored trade schools to focus on college. But we're slowly realizing that college is not what it's cracked up to be.

College tuition has risen exponentially in the past 30 years. This, coupled with the fact that attending college as an expectation, even with no plans to pay for it, leads to a vast number of people taking on student loan debt. In some cases, families put themselves in a financially tight position. In others, the students leverage their future earnings. Either way, much is riding on that education.

If a student drops out or doesn't choose the right major, it could be a long road out of debt. The schools don't do much to prevent this. On one hand, they accept kids who barely completed high school knowing they are not mentally or academically prepared for the rigors of the university. They invite them in, cash the check, and sit by as they fade away and disappear. They are left with a few semesters of memories and thousands of dollars of debt.

Then there's the long con. This affects a greater number of kids. It's the ever-increasing list of courses and majors designed to enhance the students' experiences and make them feel good about themselves, while teaching them nothing and filling the coffers of the colleges. Five years later and saddled with $80,000 in student loan debt, students discover that their degrees in Women's Studies with a concentration in dwarfism during the Elizabethan Era isn't netting the dream jobs they expected and they hardly find situations to use their specific knowledge when cold calling people to tell them they may have won a trip or discussing race relations while writing names on cups at Starbucks.

You couple this with the culture shift on college campuses we'll discuss in a later chapter and it's no wonder many parents and students are looking for alternatives. Opportunities are out there to learn a trade, to get into a company on the ground floor, or to take advantage of a niche career. But those opportunities narrow when put up against the long list of things Millennials won't do. They don't want to get up too early or work too late. They don't want to do work they feel is beneath them, even if they can learn a new skill. People used to start in the mail room of companies; today's youth would rather collect unemployment or rely on parents. Manual labor is out of the question.

Mike Rowe, host of TV shows like *Dirty Jobs* and *Somebody's Gotta Do It*, has sponsored scholarships for years with the intent of giving skills training in trades like welding and plumbing to willing high school grads. To be eligible for the scholarship, Mr. Rowe places conditions on the application process. Some are not willing to accept them. On a recent episode of *Tucker Carlson Tonight*, Mike told Tucker, "We've given away five million dollars over the last five years and yes, every year it gets increasingly difficult to affirmatively reward work ethic." He went on to suggest that there might be a link between the 'safe space movement,' and the expectations associated with it, and those who take "umbrage" with the scholarship's demands.[140]

Right now, companies all over the country are dealing with a crisis of their own, but it's not one that you might expect. They are struggling to fill their empty positions. There are an increasing number of jobs going unfilled; many with salaries greater than $50,000. Trucking companies are reporting an extreme shortage of drivers;[141] Daimler Vans Manufacturing even changed its name as a marketing ploy to get more applications.[142]States complain that they are losing potential tax revenues because these jobs aren't being filled.[143]

While these jobs do not require a college degree, they do have other requirements beyond a high school diploma. Some require months of a specific technical training, others demand difficult hours, while others are simply not that glamourous. You may be wondering, with so many people marching for $15 per hour, how there can be tens of thousands of jobs sitting unfilled that pay far more than $15? This is an interesting conundrum.

If the SJWs had their way, they would just have the wealthy subsidize those at the bottom. Their solution will make the situation worse because it doesn't get to the root of the problem. If we have people with poor work ethic and no marketable skills on one side and greedy corporate executives on the other side, how is redistribution going to fix anything? Soon those greedy executives will cut jobs and hours to maintain their wealth. When that happens, you'll have more of those low-skilled people unemployed. Now that they went from minimum wage to nothing, the income disparity will have gone up, not down.

They should stop fighting for income equality. It can never happen. There will always be innovators and inventors. Some people will also work harder than others. Those who show up, do a great job and take on more will be valued by good employers and compensated for it.

Conversely, there will be those who will do the bare minimum, make frequent errors, or be bad for business. They will make less or be relegated to part-time status. It would be more effective to spend the effort teaching people how to dress, act, speak during an interview, and how to perform if they get the job than to try to get them a salary they don't deserve.

. 5 .

Gender Inequality

I would rather trust a woman's instinct than a man's reason

– Stanley Baldwin

Of all the reasons people complain of inequality, gender inequality is the least compelling. While there may be social or cultural differences between people of different races or religions, they don't have biological or physiological differences. There is no fundamental difference between men who are black versus white, straight versus gay, or Jewish versus Muslim. The same cannot be said of women. The scope is also different. Women are not persecuted or harassed by police like minorities. They suffer from the pains of poverty but it's not a problem unique to their gender. In fact, men are more likely to be homeless or suffer from unemployment.

For all of history, men and women have behaved and been treated differently. For their part, men were the head of the household. They were expected to hunt, kill the food, and protect the family. After industrialization, men worked outside of the home to earn the money necessary to support the family. Couples shared in managing the household and disciplining the children but wives often deferred to their husbands. On the other hand, women kept the house in order, raised the children and handled the finances.

SJWs would say that these roles are societal constructs and don't have to be that way. In some ways that's true, but they don't look at the origins of these constructs. Many of the gender roles were formed out of necessity. Men, on average, are biologically stronger. This makes them better equipped to do the strenuous manual labor most jobs entailed centuries ago. Women tend to be better at nurturing and giving young children the level of emotional support they need. In other words, they have maternal instincts.

As technology advanced, tasks were automated and new jobs were created. Over time, the work became less strenuous. Women began to demand access to these jobs and started to see career opportunities they had never seen before. Studies were done and many articles and books were written to discuss the effects women in the workplace would have on the women in these new careers, as well as the men who have to work with them, but this is just one side of the coin.

While so many were celebrating this new achievement, there was something missing. To achieve a true equality of gender you can't have all of the change going one way. Where was the innovation or dramatic shift that would give men the skills to take on the traditional female roles with equal adeptness?

Men didn't become suddenly better at rearing children the moment women got jobs. What about giving birth? There is a unique bond between mother and child. How are men supposed to replicate that? Especially since they never developed the drive to do so. Excessive attention to one side with little to no attention to the other was bound to lead where it did.

Set aside single-parent homes, now we had married couples both working outside the home. They were supposedly sharing parenting duties, but this didn't happen. In most cases, the wives worked *and* managed the home. For those old enough to remember, there was a great commercial in the 1970s for Enjoli perfume that illustrates this. [144] In it, a working mom sings…

I can put the wash on the line
feed the kids, get dressed, pass out the kisses
and get to work by 5 to 9.
'Cause I'm a woman, Enjoli

I can bring home the bacon
Fry it up in a pan
And never, never, never let him forget he's a man
'Cause I'm a woman, Enjoli

This resonated because working moms could relate. Their roles hadn't changed, it just expanded. Slowly, men started to share some of the household duties. This took care of cleaning, cooking and paying bills. But what about the children? When married women started working, their husbands did not stay at home. We went from the wife being home with the children to no one being home. This may be fine for older children who spend much of their time at school but what about young children? They inevitably began to be raised by other people; people who may not have done things the way the parents did or shared their values.

This is not to say that there aren't women capable of doing these jobs or men who could do as good a job with the children. There will always be exceptions, but the term is 'gender norms' for a reason. For the vast majority of men and women, these norms have been accepted since the beginning of time. Most assumed these roles because they worked not because they were forced.

Speaking of historical norms and exceptions, those on the left who make the argument for gender equality say that just because we have certain norms doesn't make it right. They'll give you an example of a small tribe in a remote area of Africa or Asia, few people have ever heard of, where women are the dominant sex and men are submissive. What they are implying is if it works in this tribe that proves the roles can be reversed. What they don't see is that they are contradicting their own argument. Let's go to the Logic Board.

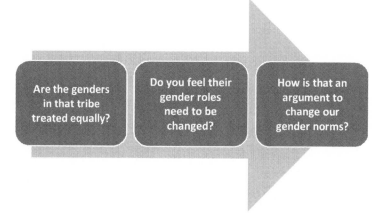

They can't answer yes to the first question because their point is that the women are dominant. If they answer yes to the second question, they are admitting they are simply disrupters out to change the norms whatever the costs. If they say no, they'd have to answer why it's okay for that tribe to operate with a dominant gender but not our culture. What we'd eventually find is that it's not so much the gender inequality they have a problem with as it is the gender experiencing the inequality.

This is one of the problems with the Left, they use extreme examples to make points that can't be proven, then use that argument to impose their will on everyone. In their view, no woman has ever been president, therefore a woman's right to be president is being suppressed. If people choose not to vote for a female candidate, even if it's simply because she's a woman, that is not gender inequality. Those who think it is inequality are promoting preference by pushing the majority of the population to change societal norms to suit their minority desires.

What happens is that many are so focused on their perceived mistreatment that they miss out on things they can do to improve their lives, the greatness of their opportunities, and the lack of similar opportunities for women throughout the world. Much of this perception is due to groups spreading a suppression narrative. They, along with the media, create several myths about how women are oppressed. Here we will examine and disprove these myths.

THE MYTH THAT MEN ARE IN CONTROL

Toxic masculinity is the new crisis in America. In the Left's fight to correct gender inequality, this is their new cause célèbre. The term is generally used to describe behavioral norms, within males, that are associated with negative actions that can lead to harmful situations. These things do exist and need to be monitored. Where they go wrong is calling it 'toxic' instead of human nature and assuming that society accepts, or in some way condones the behavior. This is a simplistic view.

It has long been acknowledged that boys are more aggressive and possess more hyper energy, on the norm, than girls. In the past, we never viewed this as a character flaw or genetic problem. At the same time, we didn't let these traits grow unshaped. When we used the term 'boys will be boys', it was understood to mean that a boy's behavior may need to be corrected but there's no cause for alarm. Men took it upon themselves to teach boys to channel and control these impulses.

This is why it is so important to have a positive male influence in a boy's life. For years, it was understood that from a certain age, a father would take his son under his wing and guide him. We also know that children learn through observing. This magnifies the importance of having positive males for them to emulate. Unfortunately, the increase of single-parent households has virtually removed this dynamic and pointing it out is viewed as sexist.

Let's look at it from another angle. No one would say it's odd for a mother to teach her daughter how to be a lady. Sharing a unique bond, and relaying wisdom about the female condition from a first-hand point of view would be looked at as beautiful, maybe even transformative. If you tell a mother, on the other hand, that her son needs the same from his father or some other positive male role model, you get a different reaction. "Are you saying I don't know how to raise my son?" may be the response.

Because of the push for gender equality and a false focus on toxic masculinity, boys are in trouble. This phenomenon has been growing for years, but it has gone largely unnoticed. Much of the attention goes to helping girls overcome inequalities that have been quickly evaporating on their own. Activists have been able to control the narrative and use faulty data to convince legislators that only the government can help girls achieve equality.

They passed laws like the Gender Equity in Education Act[145] allocating millions of dollars for training and curriculum that is girl-focused; the Carl D. Perkins Career and Technical Education Act[146]; and the far-reaching Title IX.[147] Title IX, like most legislation, was well-intentioned. But the provisions do more than level the playing field for women. Check out its effect on college sports.

No one would dispute the fact that boys are more likely to play sports than girls. If an equal number of boys and girls attend a particular college, Title IX says the participation in sports must also be equal. Since no one would suggest we force girls to play sports, the administration would be forced to reduce the number of positions for boys. This doesn't seem fair, but the reality is worse. Girls have surpassed boys in college attendance. It is not uncommon for a college to have a female population of 60%. In that scenario, only 40% of all athletes can be male. Because of situations like this, colleges are eliminating sports programs. Obviously, this was not the initial intent, but no one is doing anything to reverse it.

Most who argue for aid for girls will dismiss this by pointing out the discrepancies in the business world. They look at the percentage of men in charge of large companies, holding elected office, and other prominent positions. They see a dominant male presence and assume that this is evidence that men wield an extreme level of power and women need help. If you just look at the raw numbers, this is true, but that's only part of the story. Of course there are more men in charge, they had a 100 year head start. Women have only been in the workforce in a significant way for around 50 years. Take a closer look and you'll see the reality.

I compare the current state of women in leadership roles to the history of blacks in basketball. If you look at the NBA today, over

75% of the players are black. They are rich, powerful, and famous. Go back to the sport's origins and you'll see that all of the players were white, and it remained that way for over a decade. Through the sixties and seventies, more black players came aboard, but the league was still predominately white. If you asked owners in 1972, I'm sure none of them would have guessed the league would be dominated by black players in less than 20 years. What happened?

While the league was still white, all over the country there were black kids playing basketball and perfecting their skills at a far greater pace than whites. Much of this had to do with the low barrier to entry as compared to sports like tennis, hockey, and golf. Also, the talent pool of white athletes has a greater spread as they compete in lots of sports while blacks tend to focus on two. In any event, no one saw the shift that was coming. The same can be said about women leaders.

Girls are now outperforming boys in school. They are more disciplined, more mature, and study harder. They have exceeded boys in reading and writing for years and now, while that gap is increasing, the STEM advantage for boys is shrinking. This was happening without the benefits of charitable organizations and government programs focused on 'correcting' the gender gap in education. Those efforts just accelerated the shift.

As for boys, their performance is decreasing. They are five times more likely to be expelled than girls, more likely to drop out of high school, and less likely to attend college. Of the students that do attend college, boys earn 43% of bachelor's degrees, 40% of master's degrees and 48% of doctorates.[148] In the job market, those who see male dominance only focus on the top earners. But very few people of any gender are hedge fund managers or CEOs.

Looking across the entire spectrum of the labor force, we find that more men are discouraged workers or underemployed. In fact, contrary to the alleged pay gap discrepancy, single women without children out earn their male counterparts. Men also perform more dangerous work, so they have a greater risk of being injured at work.

Societal problems hit men harder as well. They are 3.5 times more likely to commit suicide and twice as likely to be homeless. Men represent 93% of the prison population, are five times more likely to be murdered, and eight times more likely to be a murderer than a woman. They have a shorter life expectancy, and due to flawed interpretations of masculinity, they are less likely to see a doctor regularly which leads to a greater propensity to develop health problems.

In some ways, feminists are actively participating in this demise. Like their calls of toxic masculinity, they claim that the perceived deficit for girls is a direct cause of boys and work to root it out. This creates a gender battle and boys pay the price. A 2013 study found that teachers factored behavior into grades knowing that girls behave better, causing scores for boys to go down.[149]

Next they try to suppress normative male behavior. As Christina Hoff Sommers states in her book, *The War on Boys*, "Boys today bear the burden of several powerful cultural trends: a therapeutic approach to education that valorizes feelings and denigrates competition and risk, zero-tolerance policies that punish normal antics of young males, and a gender equity movement that views masculinity as predatory. Natural male exuberance is no longer tolerated."[150]

Their final step is to erase gender differences. In 1998, the Wellesley College Center for Research on Women sponsored a teacher-training seminar entitled Gender Equity for Girls and Boys: A Conference for K-12 Teachers and Administrators. 200 teachers and administrators listened to Dr. Nancy Marshall provide nuggets of wisdom like, "A young mind is like Jell-O: you learn to fill it up with all the good stuff before it sets," and, "It's perfectly natural for a little boy to try on a skirt". The seminar further discouraged same-sex play and advised teachers to "force boy/girl mixed pairs."[151]

The bottom line is that men may have more control now, but all trends point to a change in that dynamic. The success that girls are having in school, compounded by the concerted effort of many to forcibly create change in the gender dynamic, should be enough to level the playing field over time. In fact, if the feminists have their way, there won't be genders at all. Either way, saying that men are in control is a clear overstatement. The question for those demanding gender equality is when the roles are reversed and women are in power, will they demand gender equality for boys?

THE MYTH THAT WOMEN ARE BETTER

This myth may seem odd at first. You may be thinking, "Where does he get this from?" If you think that no serious people can believe this, you're in for a surprise. If you were to do an Internet search on 'women are better,' you would find a list of articles, most taken from college studies and serious professionals, claiming that women are better at the following: Entrepreneurship, multi-tasking, marathons, and tasting wine. They are also better under pressure and better suited for success. I could go on; and these are just the articles from 2018.

Recently, in a panel discussion at the Center for American Progress Ideas Festival, NY Senator Kirsten Gillibrand argued for more female leaders saying, "If it wasn't Lehman Brothers but Lehman Sisters, we might not have had a financial collapse."[152] These arguments are not new. People have been promulgating this belief for the better part of a decade. Even Barack Obama got in on the male bashing.[153] Why do so many suddenly think that women are better than men?

Some just look at the results of years of men's actions. Men have done exponentially more bad than women throughout history. While this is true, they've also done exponentially more good. In both cases, it is mostly a matter of opportunity. If generals and CEOs are more likely to be male, then the benefits and problems created are more likely to be done by men.

The bigger driver of this argument is to increase the demand of women in leadership roles. If you can convince people that women are better, it may soften the beliefs of those who view certain roles as inherently male. We will deal with the averages in a moment, but it is important to note that when you look at the extremes, there are few performance differences among the genders.

At one extreme we have overachievers. They are creative-thinking, driven people who seem almost superhuman in their ability to achieve. They invent things, dominate sports, take the lead, and solve big problems. They often overcome great challenges. These people tend to succeed regardless of the obstacle, and this is the case for men and women.

At the other end we have bad people. Corruption, dishonesty, and evil are not traits that are confined to men; they are flaws of the human condition. These actions are individual and not gender specific. For every Martin Shkreli there's a Heather Bresch; for every Dennis Kozlowski there's an Elizabeth Holmes; for every Bashar al Assad there's an Aung San Suu Kyi; for every Kermit Gosnell there is a Jane Toppan; for every Robert Mugabe there is a Dilma Rousseff; and for every Frederick Mors there is an Amy Archer-Gilligan. Give women more opportunities to wield power and more women will respond in evil ways.

It is true that men are far more likely to do many bad things. If these actions are innate to men, then perhaps they are correct that women are better. But logic dictates there is something else at play. There are far too many variables to pinpoint why men commit more crime, but the way we treat boys may play a part.

Cultural changes have to play a part in this behavior. We discussed earlier the effects of fatherless homes. People greatly underestimate the need boys have for their fathers. This void leaves boys learning to be men through trial and error; or looking up to the wrong type of man as a role model.

Girl power also has a deleterious effect on boys. Telling girls they can do anything may seem like a good thing to do and may empower some to do great things, but it doesn't have the same effect on boys. Boys can spend their entire childhoods hearing all of the wonderful and powerful things girls can do. Where is that encouragement for them? What they get is; demands to 'calm down', requests to be 'more like your sister,' or worse, training on how *not* to be a predator.

As far as the performance differences in a given role is concerned, the best fit for any situation would depend on the skills and traits needed and the best match to those skills; regardless of gender. Women, on average, tend to be better than men at some things and worse at others. If a role calls for someone who is risk-adverse, a woman is more likely to be successful in that role than a man. Conversely, if the role calls for a linear thinker, a man may be best.

These are simplified examples based on traits most likely associated with a given gender. While they cannot predict which gender would perform better in a given situation, the same can be said for those who assert that women are better. What's worse than skewing studies or making blanket statements about men to promote women is the disregard for its effect on boys. Feminists have sons too. It is remarkable that as a group their desire to see women excel trumps their desire to see their sons treated fairly.

THE MYTH OF THE PAY GAP

For nearly a decade, we've been told that women make 77 cents for every dollar a man makes, that it's a problem, and that it proves there is systematic discrimination against women. This is not true, but it doesn't stop politicians from citing it to make political points. Former President Barack Obama made this claim not once (2013 State of the Union Address), not twice (2014 State of the Union Address), but three times in speeches.[154] In a 2015 speech at the National Press Club, Vermont Senator Bernie Sanders said, "We have to pass pay equity for women workers. It is not acceptable that women are making 78 cents an hour compared to men."[155] At least he gave them a raise.

The problem is that the claim is not true. Whether you use the census data or Bureau of Labor and Statistics data, taking all female wages and comparing them to all male wages is not a sound comparison. In these studies, doctors are not being compared to doctors, for example. Since men have been historically more apt to pursue high paying jobs, there will be more men in that pool than women. This creates an artificially high discrepancy in pay.

Even if they measured all male doctors vs all female doctors, that alone would not prove discrimination. Women are more likely to choose specialties with more flexibility like obstetrics, pediatrics, and family medicine, while men dominate cardiology, surgery, anesthesiology, and emergency medicine, disciplines that pay more. This also holds for dangerous jobs like truck drivers and drillers, and technical jobs like engineers, mathematicians, and pilots. This is more a case of self-selection than of discrimination.

This is enough to erase most but not all of the wage gap.[156] Time on the job plays a part in wage determination. Men are more likely to work long hours and take less time off. This makes it easier to move up. There are also interpersonal factors that play a part in wage discrepancies. In most cases, your salary is a negotiation, and often women are not as comfortable asking for money as men.

In 2015, actress Jennifer Lawrence penned an essay asking, "Why do I make less than my male co-stars?"[157] This after salaries were leaked in a Sony hack. She didn't blame Sony or the actors, but the implication was that it was a gender issue. When Bradley Cooper, one of her co-stars in American Hustle, offered to help his co-stars negotiate their contracts in the future, the other stars were asked if they would do the same to which Jeremy Renner famously said, "That's not my job."

Blaming sexism for not asking is wrong. In doing so, you assume that employers regularly go around offering more money than they think a particular job is worth. Another Hollywood example involves Mark Wahlberg and Michelle Williams. They were in the movie, *All of the Money in the World*, and after Kevin Spacey was removed because of his sex scandal, the starring role was recast with Christopher Plummer and some scenes needed to be reshot. Ridley Scott brought Mark and Michelle back to Europe to reshoot the scene.[158]

It was leaked that Wahlberg was paid $1.5 million while Williams received a per diem which amounted to less than $1,000. People were outraged. This was obviously an example of the gender pay gap on steroids. There's one problem with this narrative: she never negotiated. Williams told the *USA Today*, "I said I'd be wherever they needed me, whenever they needed me and they could have my salary, they could have my holiday, whatever they wanted. Because I appreciated so much that they were making this massive effort." It sounds like she was taking the hit on behalf of the #MeToo movement. Wahlberg's team negotiated.

More evidence that gender bias is not the reason for the wage gap is the fact that there aren't any women-only companies. Employers would jump at a chance to instantly lower their payroll costs by more than 20%. SJWs, having no historical perspective, say it would never happen, but it was done for years to blacks and Chinese immigrants. Today's corporate executives are no less profit-focused than they were 100 years ago.

Women are paid less, on average, than men to do the same job; however, it is nowhere near 23% (adjusted estimates are closer to

8%), and much of that difference is based on factors other than gender.[159] Factors like interview skills, college pedigree, previous salary, nepotism, references, and many others are considered for every candidate, male and female, and they skew the comparison as they are never completely identical.

There is no doubt that there is gender bias and that bias can, and often does, lead to discrimination. There is simply no evidence that the wage gap is the result of any bias. Even when it's plausible, there are simply too many variables. It is better to focus on the areas where discrimination is more likely to take place: promotions, hiring, and hostile work environment.

If a person in charge has a negative bias towards women, he is more likely to pass them over for promotion or hire less qualified men than he is to hire or promote women but pay them less. The problem for women's advocates is how to combat the problem. Government is not the answer. There is no law that can regulate the 'old boys' club.

The goal should be to minimize the negative bias. Like blacks entering a discriminatory workplace, you have to be better and overcome stereotypes. It is also important to be able to properly assess discrimination. Many SJWs see biased treatment in everything and this is simply not the case. Sometimes they find the opposite is at play.

Iris Bohnet is a behavioral economist and the director of the Women and Public Policy program at Harvard University. She wrote the book, *What Works: Gender Equality by Design*, to look at gender bias and suggest methods to combat it. In it, Bohnet crafts a detailed account of the types of bias women face as well as policies and practices that unintentionally skew against women. She then offers possible ways to get beyond these obstacles and achieve gender equality.

She referenced an experiment done to see the effects of eliminating bias in applicant selections. The results were surprising. "In 2009, the French government launched an interesting experiment that would affect all firms that made use of the services of the public employment agency, Pole Emploi. Pole Emploi invited firms to voluntarily participate in a blind recruitment process where the applicant's name, address, nationality, and picture were removed. Three economists, Luc Behaghel, Bruno Crepon, and Thomas Le Barbanchon, analyzed the impact of blind evaluations on the likelihood that members of traditionally disadvantaged groups—immigrants, children of immigrants, or residents of deprived neighborhoods—would be invited to an interview and ultimately hired. Based on a sample of 600 firms, they found a surprising result: anonymization reduced the chance that a member of a disadvantaged group received an interview and eventually was hired."[160]

The results showed that while blind evaluations remove any chance of discriminating against a candidate based on a disadvantaged group, it also prevented employers from giving candidates from disadvantaged groups' preference. In this case, that was more likely, consequently reducing employment of those in disadvantaged groups.

I applaud Mrs. Bohnet's book. It is good to make attempts to minimize gender bias. Creating programs and plans to give women the skills they may lack in relation to men is a good way to achieve this. It is also a good idea to show people their unconscious biases and teach them ways to mitigate them. My contention is that three points be maintained: the government is not used to achieve these goals, steps to aide women are not done to the detriment of men, and no unfair advantages are given to women to artificially balance the outcomes.

One area where women face clear discrimination is hostile work environment or sexual harassment in the workplace. This is unacceptable; however, there are varying degrees of harassment and the appropriate punishment needs to be meted out. In today's #MeToo environment, everyone is Harvey Weinstein. It is a good thing that this behavior is being called out, but do we want the guy who had a consensual sexual relationship with an employee treated like the guy who raped someone? Every act is not the same, and every man should not be lumped in together. This is the type of blanket judgement that leads to the constant refrain of a rape culture.

THE MYTH OF RAPE CULTURE

Like the 77-cent myth, we are constantly told that there is a rape culture on college campuses. Those making this argument cite either the Campus Sexual Assault Study, commissioned by the Department of Justice, or the AAU Climate Study on Sexual Assault and Sexual Misconduct. A quick note about surveys. Surveys can be good. You think something is a problem, so you do impartial research to confirm or refute your hypothesis. This also means that those studying an issue have a preconceived idea about it.

This is normal, even good in some cases. When researchers publish their findings objectively, that is good. If they do this even when the findings conflict with their initial beliefs, it strengthens the validity of the study (like professor Fryer's police study). It becomes a problem when they ignore data that doesn't support their claim or selectively manipulate the data to support their views. This is the case with the Campus Sexual Assault Study.[161]

There were several unmistakable problems with the way this study was done. Right in the executive summary, it states that only two universities were surveyed. Let's put that into perspective. There are over 5,000 colleges and universities in the United States. They vary in size, diversity, geography, funding type, and more. Analyzing two colleges isn't a large enough sample size to get a diverse mix. It also goes on to say that they received a large non-response rate. This is important because victims are more likely to respond. Without a sizable number of non-victim responses, you end up with a victim survey rather than a survey of the school at large. To analyze this myth, we will use the AAU study because it has a higher rate of assaults and they surveyed more schools.

The study asked the questions in a way that would illicit higher 'yes' responses. The key question that leads to the 1 in 4 claim, has to do with non-voluntary sexual contact. The goal should have been to isolate the problem and determine the cause. In the study, sexual contact was split into four categories: penetration, touching, physical force, and incapacitation. They asked questions that separated the first two from the last two. This is a problem. Penetration, which is obviously rape, is much different than touching. Also, the touching included touching a body part (wrong, but shouldn't be in a question including rape) and rubbing against you (which cannot always be contributed to sexual contact).[162]

What's worse is the latter two; the question about physical force and incapacitation. It includes, "… unable to consent or stop what was happening because you were passed out, asleep, or

142 | we want **EQUALITY**

incapacitated due to drugs or alcohol." This connotes a person who is passed out drunk, but read the quote again. Passed out is a given, but incapacitated simply means 'impaired.' This means the respondents who weren't coerced or forced, who just used bad judgment, were lumped in with those who were raped.

Another interesting take away is that the numbers are higher for TGQN (Transgender, Genderqueer or non-conforming, Questioning or Not), and twice as high for undergraduate students as it is for graduate students. Logic suggests that the numbers are drastically lower for graduate students because they are more mature, party less, and are better capable of holding their liquor. A more accurate summary of the report should be, "There's an 18–22-year-old, drinking, immaturity, and sexual experimentation culture on college campuses," something we already knew.

If the researchers were not trying to create a desired result, they would have at least measured the responses for each offense separately. Also buried in the study is the fact that only 5% of respondents said it is very likely or extremely likely that they will experience sexual assault. This is particularly low considering the amount of conversation around the topic and the much higher percentage of people reporting 'yes.' This means many of the respondents who said they were assaulted also said they were unlikely to be assaulted. Lastly, if the problem were as pervasive as many believe, there would be no co-ed colleges. No parent would knowingly put their daughter in that kind of danger.

Much of the college gender problem is a product of what the Left teaches. If a couple of 18-year-olds attend a college party, have too much to drink, and have consensual sex, should the boy be accused of rape? On most college campuses there will be an assumption of guilt even if she didn't say 'no.' Apparently, she can be too drunk to consent, but he cannot.

This dynamic cannot be good for either of them. In his case, he has spent the last 15 years of his life being told that girls are his equal. Now, with his future on the line, he's trying to understand how, if they were both drunk, he's being treated differently. For her part, it sends a bad message to create a situation where a woman has the power to flip a switch and instantly go from master, or mistress, of the universe to a shrinking violet.

The next phase of the gender inequality fight is the focus on LGBTQ rights. They claim they are discriminated against, even though this is mostly untrue. They represent less than five percent of the population, with gays and lesbians representing its most prevalent members, yet they command tremendous economic power and social influence. They dominate Hollywood as well as the fashion and art industries. They are business moguls (Tim Cook and Peter Thiel), news anchors (Anderson Cooper, Don Lemon, Rachel Maddow, and Shepard Smith) and political pundits (Sally Kohn, Charles Blow, Richard Grenell, and Guy Benson). In fact, in contrast of being an oppressed group, they are a powerhouse.

B (bi-sexual) and Q (questioning) are also not discriminated against. How can someone discriminate against a sexual preference they don't know exists? You can't look at a person and see that they are questioning. There is, however, no doubt that transgender people suffer unnecessary ridicule and disrespect. This is unfortunate but not indicative of the way most people treat them. Most people just want to mind their own business. But having someone call you names on the street shouldn't give you protected status and if they attack you physically or deny you a job because of it, there are already laws protecting you.

Everyone should have equal rights and there are no groups that are excluded from that. But for the SJWs demanding gender equality, they are not seeking equality that can be granted by law. What they want is deference. They want more female and LGBTQ representation in entertainment, business, and other mainstream areas. More than this, they want acceptance. Being allowed to live the way they want used to be enough. Now they want you to accept it, watch them openly display it, and celebrate it.

June is gay pride month. At Navy Pier, the most popular tourist attraction in the Midwest, I noticed several American flags had been replaced with gay pride flags. I posted on Facebook, "Navy Pier replaced their American flags with gay pride flags." There were several comments, most of dismay, some of support. One striking post was from a high school friend who's gay. He commented, "So much hate, wow." To give you a visual, there is a row at the end of the pier with 11 flag poles each donning the American flag. They left the American flag in the center, slightly higher than the others, and replaced the other ten with gay pride flags. So, my suggestion that maybe a 10:1 ratio is a bit much is 'hate.' This is the problem with what they disguise as equality.

And speaking of pride, I know I will lose a lot of people here, but I don't understand what people are so proud of. I take pride to mean satisfaction from one's own achievements or accomplishments. I can even see extending this to family and close friends, but outside of this small group, I just don't get it. There is no shortage of non-accomplishments of which people are willing to express their pride: black pride, gay pride, Italian pride, even American pride.

If you are born into a group, then you did not accomplish anything, therefore you have no reason to be proud. American pride is really patriotism. I love being American. I believe we have the best system of government in the world and I am impressed that our founding fathers were able to anticipate potential problems and create a process to deal with them. I know that being an American gives me a privilege few in the world can experience. But this is a vigorous support of the country, not pride.

Because of the Left's extreme definition of hate, a person who doesn't discriminate against anyone, has gay friends he dines and vacations with, works at a company where he hires and promotes gays, and defends their right to equal protection under law, is a homophobe if he also believes marriage should only be between one man and one woman.

Chicago Mayor Rahm Emmanuel famously tried to block Chick Fil-A from opening a restaurant in Chicago because, "their values are not Chicago values." [163] This because the owner supports traditional marriage. Even though the company was not being charged with discrimination, created over one hundred jobs, and was poised to bring the city much needed tax revenue; Rahm wanted to police the owner's beliefs.

So far, we've dealt with gender roles, the unfair preference given to girls, several gender equality myths, and the fight for LGBT rights, the Left's latest attempt to correct gender inequality is their push for gender fluidity. This is the charge that there is no difference between boys and girls. In fact, you can be both, neither, or 54 other genders according to Facebook. Why argue for equality of the genders when you can simply insist that gender doesn't exist. They, who charge their opponents with being anti-science, argue that gender has no innate connection, and is simply a social construct. This is a problem on many levels.

Recently a woman was thrown out of a Planet Fitness for refusing to shower in a locker room with a transgender woman.[164] At the same time, Scarlett Johansson bowed out of a movie role after backlash over her being cast to play a transgender man. The argument was that the role should have gone to a transgender actor. This is foolish. It's acting, not real life. Should poor characters only be played by poor actors? The impulse is to laugh, but creating a gender hierarchy is no laughing matter.

If we continue down this reckless path of gender confusion it will be catastrophic for children. What the SJWs are doing here is worse than demanding preference over equality, they are trying to change human nature. As Virginia Valian says in her book, *Why so Slow? The Advancement of Women*, "We don't accept biology as destiny … We vaccinate, we inoculate, we medicate … I propose we adopt the same attitude toward biological sex differences.[165]

Treating boys and girls the same is not equal. Girls, no matter how feminine, wear pants, play sports and do other things considered to be boy traits. Boys may do these things, but these actions are also normal for girls. The same cannot be said of the traditional girl activities some want to force boys to do. Encouraging boys to play dress up or to do make up when they are not asking to do so, is not allowing them to choose. Those who think that boys only act differently because we guide them to do so must not have male children.

Many of the behavioral differences between boys and girls are not taught. If the SJWs believed this, they wouldn't be trying to 'correct' this behavior out of boys. The fact that they don't see the need to correct girls' behavior is proof that there is a difference. If you give the average 4-year old boy a Barbie doll, he will wrestle with it or tear its head off. Many will say it's simply behavior that he observed, but it happens even earlier than four. Here's a story to illustrate this.

I was picking my son up from day care one day. When I arrived, he was playing with some other kids so I decided to wait a while and observe them. What I saw was a basic lesson in male/female differences. There were about eight kids in the area, half boys and half girls. The girls were sitting at a table working on some sort of crafts. The boys were running up a set of toy stairs and sliding down a slide. My son was the youngest of the four boys. Each boy would run up the stairs and climb over the boy at the top to go down the slide first. This lasted until we finally told them to stop stepping on each other. The children were between 18 months and two years old. I guarantee that my son had never seen anyone step over someone to go down a slide. Male nature needs to be focused, but it is definitely different.

For years, women have been asking if chivalry is dead, now the SJWs are saying it should be, because it's sexist.[166] Does anyone wonder how the push for the genders to be the same will affect dating or marriages in the future? These traditional male and female roles are strongest when choosing a mate. Without them, male/female relationships will be a ball of confusion.

As the next generation comes of age, they will find it difficult to navigate the dating scene. How will the SJWs differentiate themselves from those raised with traditional values? Male SJWs will alienate traditional women when they show up for their date and honk the horn so she can come out. Female SJWs will bristle when a traditional man offers to open the door or pay the check on a date. These diametrically opposed views on gender roles will limit the dating pool for both groups.

The divorce rate is already high and fewer people are marrying. These views on gender will compound this issue. Women will continue to postpone marriage until they establish their careers. As for the men, they will struggle to get a mate as the average male will be less successful than his female counterparts and women will find it hard to let go of the desire to have a mate who is her equal. Of those that do marry, the lack of gender roles will create feelings of animosity as inequality of the marital load takes its toll. All of this will lead to fewer children.

How will we maintain our society with fewer children being born? For those who believe that overpopulation is a contributor to global warming, this is a good thing. But this is in conflict with one of the SJWs greatest fights, income redistribution. Taxes are the raw materials needed to supply all of the 'entitlements' they propose. Future workers are necessary to generate income to be taxed. Look at countries like Germany, Italy, and Spain, countries the Left loves to emulate. They are aging and having fewer children. This is threatening all of their government programs, something will have to give.[167]

The bottom line is that the gender equality push is based on fallacies and misconstrued data. However, if the argument was true, the consequences would still be dire. Those who are discriminated against represent an infinitesimally small percentage of the population and we are trying to reshape a society of 330 million people to improve the lives of less than one million. I would argue that it's not improving their lives at all, but if it is, hurting millions to accomplish it is wrong. Yet, our legislators have been eager to participate in such unfair tinkering, whether it be due to ignorance or a calculated effort to advance selective achievement. Either way, they have been intentionally supporting inequality.

· 6 ·

Religion: It Sounds the Same

*At this point in my life I seriously wonder why we
have religion. I am not so sure it does more good
than harm. I think that the battle for church-state
separation has to be a continuing fight.*

—Alton Lemon

America is a country founded on Judeo-Christian principles
which are woven in the fabric of its history. A quote from
Leviticus 25:10 is inscribed on the Liberty Bell, the Declaration of
Independence speaks of "Nature's God" and rights "endowed by
our Creator …", in 1775, the Continental Congress proclaimed "a
day of publick [sic] humiliation, fasting, and prayer", 'In God We
Trust' is printed on our money, and the Holy Bible is used for
swearing in ceremonies. With this rich history of a religious
populace and 250 years of practice, you would think that this would
be the one area free from any unequal treatment; you'd be wrong.

The approach used to combat alleged religious inequalities is
different than the approach used for most other categories;
therefore, the examination has to be different as well. The way the
Left crafts their argument is ingenious. So much so that I coined a
new term to describe it: negative equality. Negative equality is
correcting a situation deemed unequal by bringing down the

advantaged group rather than raising up the disadvantaged group. This can be done by taking away from or increasing the negative treatment of the advantaged group. Here's an example of the first type of negative equality:

Let's say that two people have pie but one has a much larger slice than the other. In the typical approach to make this equal, you'd take enough pie from the person with the larger piece and give it to the person with the smaller piece to make both portions equal. With negative equality, you'd simply take from the person with the larger slice without giving the other person any, or you would take all of the pie away from both. Both actions create the same result: equal pie, but few would choose the second course of action. Here's an example of negative treatment:

There have been reports of a disproportionate number of black students being suspended and/or expelled in public schools. This has been deemed a form of inequality. In an effort to correct the problem, there are three courses of actions the administrators can take: (1) determine the root cause of the behavior and work to correct it (This is the most logical step, so they won't do it); (2) simply reduce the number of blacks being disciplined regardless of behavior (the Obama approach); or (3) discipline more white students, even if not warranted, to get their numbers up to the level of the black students. The third approach is an example of negative equality.

If you look at all of the other areas where people complain of inequality, no one suggests using negative equality to correct those imbalances. If black unemployment is too high, no one suggests firing enough whites to bring their unemployment up to the same level. If there aren't enough women in executive roles, no one suggests firing the men, without cause, until you get the gender levels to match (You could, however, say this is what the Title IX program has done to male college students).

Religion is different from all of the other areas because the SJWs are not fighting on behalf of any minority religion against a dominant one. In the previous areas we discussed, they were demanding more for blacks, Hispanics, women, the LGBT community and poor people. Here when they argue against Christianity, it's not on behalf of Jews or Muslims. What they really want is less religion. They use the guise of fighting inequality because they cannot attack Christianity head-on.

Even in our increasingly secular nation, more than 70% of Americans describe themselves as 'Christian.' I put Christian in quotes because many of them don't live in the manner the Bible dictates Christians to live. They loosely adhere to scripture, rarely read the Bible, and some say they don't pray. Their lifestyles are very different from what the typical American Christian's was just 20 years ago. I'm sure there are many books and studies as to why they still self-describe as Christian, but the important thing is they do. This tends to show itself in two ways.

On the one hand, if you make a direct charge against religion, they are likely to challenge you. However, if you simply say that a religious belief is outdated or that it causes inequality, they will likely say nothing. Because of the shift in our culture, these 'Christians' don't know whether or not the charges made against Christianity are true and are ill-equipped to mount a defense. In some cases, they side with those making the accusations. Unfortunately for many Christians, and Jews as well, leftism trumps their religion. So those who really want less religion start with a more palatable approach: inequality.

Devout Christians see this for what it is and cry foul. They say there is a war on Christianity in America. That argument is quickly shouted down by the media, fact-checkers and even fellow Christians. The problem isn't in the intent of the claim but in the intensity of the language.

The words used are important. They can gain you allies or cause you to be ignored. When Christians and supporters of traditional American values argue there's a 'war' on Christians or Christmas, they get eye-rolls and people tune them out. "It's absurd," detractors will say, "to say that the dominant religion in the country is being attacked." They are correct about the term, considering how most would define war, but not about the hostility Christians are experiencing.

When people hear 'war,' they assume it means that Christians are prohibited from practicing their religion or they are victims of a large number of physical attacks. Neither is the case; however, there is a deliberate effort to weaken Christianity in America. While calling it a war is too strong, saying Christianity is under attack is accurate. The problem is that the term 'attack' will still seem too extreme to most. Perhaps the best way to fight back without being accused of being hyperbolic is to call it a calculated smear campaign.

The first example of inequality is the dominance of Christianity. They feel that America, being a Christian majority nation, does not exhibit equality for all religions and therefore needs to be changed. Celebrating Christian holidays marginalizes other religions and religious expressions in public is discriminating to non-believers.

But take a closer look at their argument. Those saying the dominance of Christianity is unfair are not calling for increased representation of Judaism or Islam. What they want is to bring the public displays of Christianity down to the levels of the other major religions, virtually non-existent. In other words, minimizing Christianity under the guise of equality gets them closer to their actual goal, less religious influence on American culture.

There are two problems with their equality argument. The first is constitutional. In many areas, the constitution's brilliance is in its brevity. The Establishment Clause, like the 2nd amendment, has caused heated debates on its interpretation. People often add words that are not there to try to make their argument. The clause simply says, "Congress shall make no law respecting an establishment of religion, or prohibiting the free exercise thereof …" This has largely happened with no interference, but those seeking equality disagree.

Those arguing against Christianity are confused as to the definition of 'establishment' of religion. They mistakenly think that free to exercise means equal amount of exercise. If the majority of the country practices the same religion, obviously the religious expression you see will not be equal. But unlike many countries, we do not have a state religion.

Take a moment to read the clause again. It says *Congress* shall make no law. This is critical to the argument because it proves the intent was not to limit any desires of the people, only to prevent Congress from mandating religious acts. Earlier we discussed Spain and Rome's laws against blasphemy and heresy. This is an example of establishing a religion. However, if Congress decided to decorate the Capital from end to end with Christmas decorations and Bible scripture, it would not violate this portion of the 1st amendment. If you disagree, I'd ask you to tell me what law Congress established surrounding the decorations.

The other problem with their argument is that it comes dangerously close to prohibiting the free exercise of religion. Many countries have majority cultures and with it, majority religions. The majority in India practice Hinduism; in Cambodia and Thailand, it's Buddhism. The majority of African countries, with the exception of those in northern Africa, practice Christianity; and the majority of the Middle East practices Islam.

It is safe to say that when the majority of the citizens of a country have similar cultural practices, including religious ones, those practices will permeate throughout the society. No one in their right mind would go to a Muslim majority country and try to remove Islam from the culture. The same should go for those in America. Unfortunately, the anti-religion crowd cannot allow that influence on the culture to continue.

They've made several challenges against religion in society in the last 50 years. While they weren't successful in the majority of cases, they were in an alarmingly high percentage of them. Even when they lose, they win; moving the needle ever-so-slightly towards their goal.

Their biggest win, as it was a direct run at religion, was the Supreme Court's 1962 decision to strike down prayer in schools. In *Engels v. Vitale*, it was deemed unconstitutional, in a 5-4 decision, for New York public school students to open the school day reciting the "Regent's Prayer." This, even though the prayer in question didn't promote a particular religion. Here is the prayer they recited:

"Almighty God, we acknowledge our dependence upon Thee, and we beg Thy blessings upon us, our parents, our teachers, and our Country."

At its core, the decision seems flimsy. The prayer was not specific to any religion, was voluntary, and was not created through legislation. The prayer did mention God, which some would argue narrows the list of religions it could be referencing, but the first amendment doesn't say 'you have a right not to hear someone else say God.' At the time, most assumed there was an easy fix. Just have a moment of prayer every morning but no specific prayer and everything would be fine. Not surprisingly, this case was used as a precedent to prevent that and other religious actions at schools as well as colleges and universities.

In 1971, the Supreme Court heard the case of *Lemon v. Kurtzman.* The key takeaway here was that the justices established, seemingly out of thin air, the 'Lemon Test.' This created a three-prong test to determine if a law violates the Establishment Clause. The three prongs are as follows:

1. *The statute must have a secular legislative purpose.*
2. *The principal or primary effect of the statute must not advance nor inhibit religion.*
3. *The statute must not result in an "excessive government entanglement" with religion.*

This test is highly problematic for two reasons: (1) For a group tasked with maintaining the integrity of the Constitution, it seems odd that the justices would create their own criteria using a baseline that virtually adds meaning to the Constitution that simply doesn't exist. (2) The first part of the test gives every law pertaining to religion a built-in reason for constitutional challenge. It inherently strengthens the Establishment Clause and weakens the free expression portion of the amendment. How can any law protecting free expression have a 'secular purpose'? What is the secular purpose in allowing prayer in school, blue laws on Sundays, or a Jew to wear a yarmulke when in his military uniform?

Put plainly, there will always be a secular purpose for denying these laws and never a secular purpose for approving them. This began the diminution of free expression of religion. Each challenge and eventual win by the SJWs has come based on the Lemon test. What's worse, most of the wins claimed by those fighting for religious freedom did not come from passing the Lemon test. In most cases, the justices simply chose to ignore their own test. This means they could change their minds on a whim. Let's look at some of the cases decided after this highly suspect Lemon Test.

In 1980, the court struck down a Kentucky law mandating the display of the Ten Commandments in classrooms because it had no secular purpose (*Stone v. Graham*). In 1983, the Nebraska legislature was sued for opening each of its sessions with a prayer. To complicate matters, the person leading the prayer was a chaplain and he was paid with public funds. The court ignored their own test, which the prayer clearly violated, and upheld the constitutionality of the prayer due to the "long historical custom of the practice" (*Marsh v. Chambers*). In 1984, the court heard a case where Rhode Island was accused of violating the Establishment Cause by including a nativity scene in a public park. The court ruled that, "notwithstanding the religious significance of the creche, the city of Pawtucket has not violated the Establishment Clause of the first amendment." Oddly claiming that the law passed the three-pronged test (*Lynch v. Donnelly*).

As was inevitably the case, the court started to come up with mixed decisions in spite of the clear-cut Lemon test. In *Wallace v Jaffree* (1985), they determined that Alabama's law authorizing a period of silence for "meditation or prayer" did not pass the test. So much for the belief that a moment of silence would have been the solution to the school prayer issue. In *Estate of Thorton v. Caldor, Inc* (1985), it was determined that giving employees the right not to work on their chosen Sabbath violated the Establishment Clause.

In *County of Allegheny v. ACLU* (1989), it was deemed unconstitutional to display a nativity scene at Pittsburgh's city display, but it did not violate the Establishment Clause for the state of Texas to display a monument inscribed with the Ten Commandments (*Van Orden v. Perry 2005*). In *Lee v. Weisman* (1992), the court deemed clergy-led prayer at graduations unconstitutional. In 2000, they determined that it was unconstitutional for students to lead a student group in prayer at football games. The school district allowed it; the court overturned it (*Sante Fe Independent School District v Doe*).

In *Locke v. Davey* (2004), Washington state's decision to not award scholarship funds to college students pursuing devotional divinity degrees was deemed constitutional. And finally, in *Christian Legal Society v. Martinez* (2010), the Supreme Court ruled 5–4 in favor of the Hasting College of Law. In this case, the Hastings College of Law at the University of California denied the Christian Legal Society's recognition as a student organization because it required its members to agree to a 'Statement of Beliefs.'

You are free to agree or disagree with the decisions of these cases. The problem the Lemon Test caused is obvious. There is no 'secular purpose' to open a legislative session with a prayer, allow observance of a chosen Sabbath, or to allow the use of hoasca or peyote, yet all of these actions were upheld. This has made it more onerous for religious freedoms to be protected and easier to challenge them. And depending on who gets to make future appointments, it's likely to get more difficult for those fighting to maintain those freedoms.

While the Left was carefully crafting their legal challenges, they had an area where they could have even greater impact, the culture. With their attacks meeting little to no resistance, there was unlimited potential and they took full advantage of it.

First, they tried to secularize Christmas. While the Supreme Court was hearing cases about nativity scenes, the secular progressives were challenging municipalities throughout the country to allow alternative displays. Atheists and those worshiping the occult wanted equal displays. Then they pressured companies to stop allowing their employees to say, "Merry Christmas." They claimed "Happy Holidays" was more inclusive. But inclusive to what? The holiday is uniquely Christian. Many will say it's not a big deal, but who is making it a big deal?

It's logical to assume that if 70% of the country identifies as Christian and the majority of those who don't aren't bothered by the sentiment, saying "Merry Christmas" will generally be accepted. It's those who rail against wishing others Merry Christmas that are making it a big deal. And yet, it seems that at some point, trying not to offend morphed into deferring to an extremely small percentage of the population.

Next, they used propaganda to shift the attitude of the public. Journalist focused on stories that made Christians seem intolerant or racist. Turn on any TV program and they are bound to have an episode displaying religious people, mostly devout Christians, as cult leaders, child abusers, white supremacists, serial killers, anarchists, and racists. They are close-minded zealots who reject science and hate the government. This is how Hollywood views Christians and how they want you to view them.

Twenty-six years ago, Sinead O'Connor famously tore a photo of Pope John II during a *Saturday Night Live* performance; at least she was vilified by many. Today, celebrities get bonus points for mocking Christianity. Miley Cyrus slammed Christians for believing the story of Noah's ark and went on to say those who believe in traditional marriage should not be able to make laws. Joy Behar of the View mocked Vice President Pence for speaking to God. Larry David urinated on a picture of Jesus in an episode of *Curb Your Enthusiasm*. Stephen Colbert said, "I grew up in a cult too!" speaking about Catholicism in an interview with Rose McGowan.

At the movies, they take one of two approaches, they mock Christians or they take the Word out of context. Movies like *Rapture-Palooza* and *This is the End* reference the Bible in a comedic attempt to minimize its message, make the prophesies seem absurd and to take every word literally; in a farcical manner. Other movies like *Noah* and *Gods and Kings* profess to tell the story without mocking religion directly. While this is a step up, they tend to focus more on action and drama than the religious component. They become riveting stories of fiction whose message is lost. It's also telling that both movies were directed by Atheists.

Russell Crowe, who plays Noah in the movie, had this to say about his character:

"The funny thing with people, they consider Noah to be a benevolent figure because he looked after the animals: 'Awww, Noah. Noah and the animals.' It's like, are you kidding me?" he says with a laugh. "This is the dude that stood by and watched the entire population of the planet perish."[168]

For those who see the legal battles and the cultural shift and think it doesn't matter, look at what has happened in the last 50 years. The schools have gotten demonstrably worse, crime reached new heights, chivalry died, and common courtesy was replaced by the me generation. Open promiscuity, especially of women, and acceptance of drug use became the norm. Things people would have only done or said in private 50 years ago they do in front of cameras now.

Many would say that the loss of religion in our culture has nothing to do with it. They will have a hard time defending that argument. Even those who don't believe would have to say that the Bible teaches morals and good behavior. Without God, where would we get our morals from? They'd just be whatever one feels and feelings can change. There is no way that having God be ubiquitous in society for generations then disappearing into the shadows in thirty years can have anything but a disastrous effect.

The anything goes attitude has led to more poverty, single-parent households, homelessness, mental illness, and crime. Art imitates life, so the media and entertainment constantly portray the ugly side of society on a loop. It has now soaked into the fabric of our culture. This has led to the only logical conclusion, politicians crafting policies in an attempt to help alleviate these problems. As well-intentioned as they are, they can't fix behavior and, what's worse, we end up losing freedom as their new laws don't conform to the Constitution, but our desperation allows them latitude.

Progressives will read this and accuse me of being another Christian whining with no cause for alarm. Let's look at this another way. Of the three major religions, Christianity, Islam, and Judaism, are they treated equally in America? The answer is clearly no. In media, Christianity is challenged as aggressive, Islam is generally protected from alleged Christian attacks, and Judaism goes mostly ignored.

Feel free to think religion is fantasy and is constantly used to condone bad behavior. This has nothing to do with the fact that Christianity is singled out. It is often said that the Bible is full of murder, wars, and bad acts. Some still use slavery or the Crusades as a justification of the dangers of Christianity. These people are either ignorant or deliberately overlooking the facts. But their argument proves my point of inequality. 300 years of slavery proves Christians are bad, but not 1,300 years of slavery by the Arab Caliphates. Christians were wrong for the Crusades but Muslims weren't wrong for conquering most of the Middle East.

Take a moment and think about each religion. Ignore, for the moment, the theological differences and focus on the text each religion holds sacred: *The Holy Bible* and the *Quran*. Now compare the teachings of each to the shift in culture the Left is promoting. It is hard to dispute that this cultural shift goes against each religion, not just Christianity. Let's look at how some of the areas those seeking equality focus on and see what each religion says about them.

WOMEN

The Holy Bible

The women of Zion are haughty, walking along with outstretched necks, flirting with their eyes, strutting along with swaying hips, with ornaments jingling on their ankles. Therefore the Lord will bring sores on the heads of the women of Zion; the Lord will make their scalps bald. (Isaiah 3:16-17)

Women should remain silent in the churches. They are not allowed to speak, if they want to inquire about something, they should ask their own husbands at home; for it is disgraceful for a woman to speak in the church. (1 Corinthians 14:34)

The Quran

Men are the maintainers of women, with what Allah has made some of them to excel others and with what they spend out of their wealth. So the good women are obedient, guarding the unseen as Allah has guarded. And (as to) those on whose part you fear desertion, admonish them, and leave them alone in the beds and chastise them. So if they obey you, seek not a way against them. Surely Allah is ever Exalted, Great. (4:34)

SEXUALITY

The Holy Bible

If a man has sexual relations with a man as one does with a woman, both of them have done what is detestable. (Leviticus 20:13)

Because of this, God gave them over to shameful lusts. Even their women exchanged natural sexual relations for unnatural ones. In the same way the men also abandoned natural relations with women and were inflamed with lust for one another. Men committed shameful acts with other men, and received in themselves the due penalty for their error. (Romans 1:26-27)

The Quran

And go not nigh to fornication: surely it is an obscenity. And evil is the way. (17:32)

Will you come to men lustfully rather than women? Nay, you are a people who act ignorantly. (27:55)

If two men among you are guilty of lewdness, punish them both. If they repent and amend, leave them alone; for Allah is Oft-returning, Most Merciful. (4:16)

CAPITAL PUNISHMENT

The Holy Bible

Whoever sheds human blood, by humans shall their blood be shed; for in the image of God has God made mankind. (Genesis 9:6)

But if anyone schemes and kills someone deliberately, that person is to be taken from my altar and put to death. Anyone who attacks their father or mother is to be put to death. Anyone who kidnaps someone is to be put to death, whether the victim has been sold or is still in the kidnapper's possession. (Exodus 21:14-16)

The Quran

As for the thief, both male and female, cut off their hands. It is the reward of their own deeds, an exemplary punishment from Allah. (5:38)

Believers, in case of murder, the death penalty is the sanctioned retaliation: a free man for a free man, a slave for a slave, and a female for a female. However, if the convicted person receives pardon from the aggrieved party, the prescribed rules of compensation must be followed accordingly. This is a merciful alteration from your Lord. Whoever transgresses against it will face a painful punishment. (2:178)

They each talk about providing charity and helping the poor but this help comes from the believers, not the government. They also both speak of treating people the same regardless of status. The rich are chided for taking advantage of the poor but the poor should not be shown favor.

SHARIA

Sharia, or Islamic law, is a list of guiding principles used by Muslims to maintain adherence to the Quran. It is often compared to theology for Christians. Some Muslim-majority countries base their laws on Sharia, while others do not. There has been controversy over the laws some follow as well as whether or not the laws should be allowed in the west. Here are some examples:

- Theft is punishable by amputation of the hands.
- Criticizing or denying any part of the Quran, Muhammad, or Allah is punishable by death.
- A Muslim who becomes a non-Muslim is punishable by death.

- A non-Muslim man who marries a Muslim woman is punishable by death.
- A woman or girl who has been raped cannot testify in court against her rapist(s).
- A woman or girl who alleges rape without producing 4 male witnesses is guilty of adultery.
- A woman or girl found guilty of adultery is punishable by death.
- A male convicted of rape can have his conviction dismissed by marrying his victim.
- Muslim men have sexual rights to any woman/girl not wearing the Hijab.
- A divorced wife loses custody of all children over 6 years of age or when they exceed it.
- Muslims should engage in Taqiyya and lie to non-Muslims to advance Islam.

Whatever your thoughts on Islam, there is also a stark difference in how Christianity is treated vs Islam. Here's an example of how Sharia Law was defended in Huff Post and CNN articles. In the *Huffington Post* article, the writer gave no info about Sharia Law. Instead, she said things like, "It's a personal relationship," "Asking someone not to believe in Sharia Law is a blatant violation of religious freedom," and "It's not all about punishment."[169] Doesn't that mean it's partially about punishment? She should have at least mentioned something specific about the laws.

The CNN article did the same thing. This is what they do. They deflect, excuse, or make a false equivalence with Christianity. In the

Huffington Post article, the writer includes a tweet from 'Christian' columnist and blogger Rachel Held Evans which read, "Deuteronomy 21:18–21 calls for stoning disobedient children. Want to deport "all people who believe the Bible now?"

I'd like to respectfully ask her to produce a case where a Christian parent stoned his or her child for being disobedient, not in recent history, ever. I'd have no problem producing a case where: people were killed for criticizing Muhammad (Charlie Hebdo)[170], a woman found guilty of committing adultery being killed (Aisha Ibrahim Duhulow; though she was actually raped),[171] and genital mutilations (millions).

What's important for our purposes is not how many Muslims practice these laws or how stringently they are enforced. The comparison of note here is how the laws are treated in relation to other religions. In the HuffPost and CNN articles, the writers looked to minimize the impact of Sharia law on Muslims in the west, dismiss any violence or inequalities in the Sharia as myths, and to dismiss those critical of Sharia as racist.[172] One must simply ask, if Christians had similar laws, would these writers defend them?

JIHAD

Finally, it is important to address Islamists and their continued jihad against non-Muslims. There is a lot of rhetoric on both sides. Those on the left dismiss it as a small, isolated problem. Like the Sharia example above, they tend to highlight the positive and downplay obvious dangers. On the right, they exaggerate the number of Muslims who are willing to kill innocents in the name of Islam. While far too many are amenable to the actions, that is different than participating. They also conflate verses of the Quran to suggest that it condones violence, without context.

I am by no means an authority on Islam or the Quran, but I've read these alleged 'jihad verses' and, in context, the vast majority of them are speaking of actions to be taken toward those who wage war against Islam. Several others speak of what will happen to those who go against Allah but doesn't reference anything the reader should do first hand. Even verses that may seem to invoke violence like, "Fight those who do not believe in Allah, nor in the latter day, nor do they prohibit what Allah and His Messenger have prohibited, nor follow the religion of truth, out of those who have been given the Book, until they pay the tax in acknowledgment of superiority and they are in a state of subjection," (9:29) and, "So do not follow the unbelievers and strive against them a mighty striving with it," (25:52), may be figurative rather than literal.

All of this is immaterial when reviewing the difference that truly matters. What the religious text commands is less important than how it is interpreted by its adherents. It's impossible to know, but if we assume a mere 1% of Muslims believe the Quran commands them to commit jihad against non-believers, that's over 10 million people. What is the numbers for Christians? An honest observer would have to say it's close to zero, or at most, tens of people.

In defending Jihadists, those on the left get creative. When they're not reaching back hundreds of years to point out the Crusades or slavery in America, they point to attacks by white supremacists. For instance, Dylan Roof, the terrorists who killed nine parishioners at a black church in South Carolina was used as an example of Christian extremists. These attempts are laughable.

First, if Dylan Roof is a Christian, so were the members of the church. It's dubious at best to assume all white supremacists are Christians. More importantly, is the fact that with the exception of the Army of God and a couple of radical anti-abortionists, none of these people claim they are killing in the *name* of Jesus Christ. The jihadists, on the other hand, make that very claim, moments before the attack, no matter how skewed their belief is.

Worse, even if all of the white supremacist attacks were in the name of Jesus, the numbers would dwarf the attacks committed by jihadists. Yet the religious disdain in the mainstream media is heavily skewed against Christians. This is hard evidence of the lack of equality.

Whether you are talking about same-sex marriage, gender roles, faith, crime, sexual behavior, capital punishment, or government oversight, all three religions have similar beliefs. Of course, you can find some religious leader who preaches against the doctrine, but the text, and most adherents, have beliefs that are vastly different than the progressives. So why are Christians the only ones attacked for their beliefs? The logic board portends there may be bias involved:

| Are traditional male roles wrong? | Is it wrong to be against same-sex marriage? | Christians, Jews, and Muslims all preach this | Why are Christians only attacked? |

One reason is simply because they are the easiest target. They are the most vocal and disliked religion of the three. Also, since they are the majority, no one is worried about being accused of discrimination. But it's deeper than that. The Left's views on Islam is interesting. Based on the aforementioned quotes from the Quran and the large percentage of Muslims who practice or affirm Sharia Law, you'd think their beliefs would be antithetical to the goals of the Left. Why then, do they advocate on behalf of Muslims rather than attack them like they do Christians?

On the surface this seems odd but it's a calculated risk. The Left knows how to fight. They have simply surmised that it is easier to defeat their opponents if they are not unified. Creating fraction between the religions and within different sects of each religion minimizes the opposition to their goals. If they can create a rift between Christians and Jews, or Christians and Muslims, each religion will be weakened, they hope, and they will be less likely to coalesce over their shared disdain for the Left.

This position is even more beneficial from a political perspective. If Republicans are being tough on immigration and focusing on Islamic terror, Democrats see a tactical advantage in convincing people they are intolerant. What better way than to lobby for refugees from majority Muslim countries? The numbers are so small that it doesn't matter that their culture is in complete conflict with their leftist goals.

This is how those on the left could scream and organize protests because there were no women nominated for best director at the Oscars but remain silent about abused women not being allowed to divorce in Australia,[173] women not being able to drive a car in Saudi

Arabia,[174] honor killings in Pakistan,[175] or other cases of women's rights being suppressed throughout the world.

This is a great example of the hypocrisy of the Left. The group that often speaks of protecting and respecting the culture of others doesn't demand the same for American culture. Many will say they are not attacking the culture, but their actions prove them wrong.

There is a unique dynamic at play that explains why the Jews are not attacked by the Left. Like black conservatives, Jewish conservatives are a small percentage of the Jewish community. Therefore, nothing would be gained by attacking them. As for secular Jews, most have the same goal as the SJWs; a secular America.

Why attack Jews if the majority of those with political power (Bernie Sanders, Rahm Emmanuel, and Chuck Schumer), money and influence (Jeff Zucker, Paul Krugman, and George Soros), and entertainment cache (Woody Allen, Steven Spielberg, and Natalie Portman) are lending their money and influence to the cause? Think Leon Trotsky. While the majority of Jews still maintain traditional American values, many in line with those of Christian conservatives, what they *say* aligns with the Left's ideology, so they get a pass.

What is clear is that the argument against traditional Christian values has nothing to do with equality. Furthermore, everyone needs to understand that if the secular progressives defeat mainstream Christianity, the Jews and Muslims will go next, along with the soul of the nation.

· 7 ·

Trump: Fascists, Fake News, and the Future of America

The media's the most powerful entity on earth.
They have the power to make the innocent guilty
and to make the guilty innocent, and that's power.
Because they control the minds of the masses.

— Malcolm X

In previous chapters, I made the argument that those demanding equality are actually promoting actions that cause inequality. Further, the destruction of traditional norms and the cultural shift to the left have exacerbated the problems they are trying to fight. As a society, our focus has shifted from inputs to outcomes. Many of the problems we blame on racism, sexism, and class warfare are simply the result of individual actions; whether it be poor choices or bad decisions.

Up to this point, I avoided the elephant in the room; Donald Trump. This was by design. My primary focus is always the cultural shift that is hurting the country and why all of the effort to create equality seems to be in vain. This was here before the current president, and will be here long after; however, the efforts have vastly increased since Trump's election. It is impossible to discuss the extremes to which the cultural and political climates have gone without addressing President Trump.

There was a period when people started to realize that the tactics of the Left were not working. Some still believed what they said, regardless of the many examples to the contrary. Others realized their plans didn't work, but were okay with them either because they believed the plans were well-intentioned or because they were members of a group that benefited from the plans. However, there was a growing number of people who realized that these demands were empty or would lead to unfavorable results.

Just when logic started to have an impact, the Left found ways to counter it. First, there was the election of President Obama. His election created such a euphoria that people expected everything to improve. When it didn't, conservatives got excited. Now, they thought, people will understand liberal policies don't work. They underestimated the adoration of Obama. He told people we just needed to do more, or give it time, or better, it's because of Republican opposition that progress wasn't being made. People ate it up.

What he said didn't comport with reality, but the media was reluctant to call him out on it, some because they supported his policies others because they didn't want to be called racist. Republicans, for their part, grappled with how to address him. In the past, they would attack the Democrats without reservation. This changed with Obama because like the media, they didn't want to be labeled as racists.

This created a strange dichotomy. Obama was loved but his policies weren't. While he was seemingly untouchable, other Democrats didn't share this luxury. When Obama was elected,

Democrats controlled both houses of Congress. In the 2010 midterm elections, they lost control of the house; in 2014 they would also lose the senate.[176] [177]Republicans would go on to control 32 of the 50 governorships and state legislatures.

As Obama's presidency wound down, both parties needed a reset. Looking at recent election history, they both had reason for concern. For Republicans, they had only won the popular vote once in the last six national elections, and that was 12 years earlier. For Democrats, they were hemorrhaging power on the state level. They only controlled 26% of the nation's state legislatures. How could these things take place at the same time? One would think they were mutually exclusive. The truth lies in how people view the government.

People aren't constitutional scholars and most only pay attention to issues that affect them directly and what they see in the news. Because of this, they don't view national politics as being connected to local politics. For national elections, most tend to vote for the person they like the most. For local and state elections, they want to know how things will affect them. This is how people can vote for Obama who, for instance, supports higher taxes, then vote for the congressional candidate who wants to lower taxes.

They view the president as setting a tone. They want someone who inspires, gives hope, consoles, and shows empathy. For their state representative and councilman, they want someone who will deliver results. Nowhere does this have a bigger impact than in the independent vote. Most partisans will vote for the party candidate even if they dislike him, but independents are not loyal to a party. Add to this the fact that in 2016, more people identified as independent than did those who identified as Democrat or Republican, and the parties had reason for concern.

Republicans had a large group of qualified candidates, but none of them had a simple, concise message the average voter could relate to, and the Democrats did not know how they would fare without a charismatic, black candidate at the top of the ticket. No one was prepared for what we were about to get: Hillary Clinton and Donald Trump.

Though the road for each was completely different—she, the heir apparent; he, a dark horse—neither party was happy with their primary winner. Clinton came with years of baggage, and Trump was too unconventional. He turned people off, made rookie mistakes, and was always in attack mode. That would be his strength in the end. What many Republican voters saw, that the elites in the party still don't see, was that Trump was willing to fight. Though it often came in ways they didn't condone, they were tired of Republicans who retreated whenever they were attacked.

This was not enough for Trump to win however, he needed Clinton to help, and she offered it in spades. She ran her campaign like she had already won. She neglected key battleground states, attacked Trump's supporters rather than the candidate, and never developed a cohesive message. In that respect, she suffered the same fate as Trump's primary opponents. Think what you will about his message, but it was clear: fix immigration, reduce regulations, cut taxes, and repeal Obamacare. Clinton's message: "I will be the first female president and my opponent's a racist."

Trump's win shocked the nation. It's too soon to see what the long-term effects will be, but initially, his win was a boon for both parties. The Republicans, at least temporarily, won the ability to stop the expansion of leftist federal policies. When Obama lost Congress, he started to govern by executive fiat, signing executive orders to implement changes he'd never get Congress to pass legislatively. This gave Republicans an instant mandate to at least undo some of his executive orders and to possibly reign in the federal government. They also should have found hope in the election results.

Much was made of the fact that, yet again, the Republicans lost the popular vote. However, Trump alienated many Republicans. Some popular pundits, like George Will and Joe Scarborough, left the party.[178] Many others declared themselves never-Trumpers and either asked their followers to vote for Hillary or a third-party candidate. With horrendous media coverage and fellow Republicans actively campaigning against him, Trump lost the popular vote by three million votes. This difference is less than the Libertarian candidate received, who, it's safe to assume, was the candidate of choice for never-Trumpers.[179] This means there were more people open to conservative principles than Republicans thought.

Democrats were helped because they had no direction without Barack Obama. Their push to legislate perceived inequalities through preference was losing at the ballot box, and screaming "Racist!" at every turn was losing its luster. Trump's election changed all of that. The hyper-emotional, angry political climate that developed during the campaign increased after the election. Every day someone on the left says that we all must resist because our freedoms are being stripped away. I defy anyone to list one freedom that has been lost since Trump's inauguration.

Journalists write stories that support these claims. They suggest, without evidence, that gay rights, voting rights, and women's reproductive rights are under attack. They highlight stories that help the Left's narrative and suppress stories that present the other side. But this is not indicative of the realities on the ground. There are no freedoms Americans had on 1/19/2017 that have disappeared 18 months later. Gays can still marry, blacks can still vote, and women can still get abortions. Illegals still flood into the country, only now they have attorneys.[180]

Just like the false loss of freedom narrative, there has been constant cries of fascism aimed at Trump and his administration. Those who call Trump a fascist just show that they don't know what fascism is. The Merriam Webster dictionary defines fascism as a political philosophy, movement, or regime (such as that of the Fascisti) that exalts nation and often race above the individual and that stands for a centralized autocratic government headed by a dictatorial leader, severe economic and social regimentation, and forcible suppression of opposition.

It's silly that this is even a serious topic of conversation. Obviously, people are focusing solely on the nationalism part and saying that 'Make America Great Again' is extreme nationalism. They also extrapolate that into exalting race. This is a stretch, but I'm willing to give them this overreaching argument because they are still far from proving fascism. Nationalism alone does not a fascist make. In fact, if you look closely at the definition, there is a political philosophy alive in America today that resembles fascism; and it's not on the right.

EXALTS THE NATION AND OFTEN
RACE ABOVE THE INDIVIDUAL

Ask yourself, to whom does this attribute fit? The media and entertainment industries will have you believe it's the Right. This is a fallacy. It's the Left for whom race is paramount. They count the number of minorities in high-profile jobs, create campaigns to demand more blacks are nominated for awards, and go on TV and openly announce, "I always root for the black people."

They swoon over multiculturalism, intersectionality, and black-brown coalitions. They elevate everything black or Hispanic while reminding everyone of the dangers of whites, particularly straight white males. They complain of cultural appropriation by whites and make lists of things white people should not do.

White liberals are the biggest purveyors of the race-focused movement from the Left. They write articles hoping for white men to be killed and are eager to tell blacks that they understand the struggle they go through. They teach courses on white privilege and promote the false narrative that blacks cannot be racist. These moves have given blacks a sort of super social status. They can do or say nearly anything without repercussions.

This has emboldened them to traffic in open racism. They talk about the immoral traits innate to whites and joke about killing white people. From Louis Farrakhan to CNN's Michaela Angela Davis, racist, vile, and demeaning things are constantly said about whites and no one says a word.

While virtually everything about the Left revolves around race, what is the charge of Trump? Making comments about Mexicans and immigrants. Any fair-minded person will admit he was talking about illegals. You can still disagree with him, but it's not racist if it doesn't include members of the race that are here legally. This is also different from exalting a race. He has made no comments about elevating any race above another, Aryan or otherwise.

CENTRALIZED AUTOCRATIC GOVERNMENT

Donald Trump is no autocrat; an autocrat has supreme power. If he was an autocrat, he would not have such a hard time getting his agenda advanced. There would be a wall along the US-Mexican border, Obamacare would have long been repealed, the tax reform bill would have been bigger, and the Republicans would have won all of the special elections held since he took office.

SEVERE ECONOMIC AND SOCIAL REGIMENTATION

Severe economic controls could be a campaign slogan for the Left. They want the government to run the economy, and they want to run the government. Most on the left can be categorized into two groups: those who claim to be capitalists but want heavy regulations on every facet of business and high taxes, and those who want to put an end to capitalism. In other words, those who want to be de facto owners of production and those who want to own production.

Social control on its face seems like a right-wing trait. They are the ones who tend to speak of morality and lament, like me, the declination of the culture. The difference is we don't want to legislate it. Outside of abortion, of which remaining passive while babies are murdered is a bridge too far for many, conservatives are not trying to make any social acts they find immoral a crime. They just take offense to the Left openly promoting those acts.

The Left, on the other hand, creates marketing campaigns for salacious behavior. They claim we're a democracy. If so, with their celebrity cohorts and entertainment acting as propaganda, they should sell their ideas to the American people. That's the way our system works. The problem is, when they don't get the votes necessary, they protest, call their opponents racists, and petition the courts.

FORCIBLE SUPPRESSION OF OPPOSITION

While the fascist definition calls for suppression by force, that force doesn't have to be physical. One can weaken his opponent through threats and intimidation. Where is the evidence of this with President Trump? Some will say his attacks on the media are evidence of suppression. While I think his attacks should be more precise, it's hardly suppression. Not only are they free to attack him, they do it at an unprecedented rate. It is the media's job to hold him accountable, but not actively facilitate his demise. However, this is exactly what they are trying to do.

The day after his inauguration, hundreds of thousands of women marched in every major city in the country. Celebrities in attendance made some vile, threatening comments; nothing happened. People have mock assassinated Trump and attacked, ridiculed, sued, and threatened him, his family, and his cabinet; yet no one's been arrested.

In contrast, look at the Left. First there is the media, of which they have nearly full control. Trump is wrong, or at least imprecise (a trait that is unfortunately common for him), when he says the media is fake news. Perhaps that would be better as it would be easier to debunk. What they are is dishonest, misleading, agenda-driven, and spiteful.[181]

Many of their negative stories fall into one of five categories: (1) factual, but taken out of context; (2) undermining their point; (3) lies; (4) hypothetical crimes; and (5) crazy. With the heightened hysteria surrounding Trump for the last two years, there are thousands of examples. I will briefly list a few, in order, to highlight each type of story.

1. Trump dishonors Japan by dumping an entire box of fish food.

2. Running an article stating Trump said something then linking a video showing he didn't.

3. Time magazine cover of little girl 'taken' from her mother.

4. Making up hypothetical things that may be in Trump's taxes, then analyzing the legal problems this 'made-up' tax info would cause him.

5. Example that Trump is like Hitler – Hitler claimed the Jews declared war on Germany; Trump said Barack Obama wasn't born in the US.

The bottom line is that the media uses its platform as effectively as Trump. They make up stories, bury successes, and underhandedly pass opinion off as news. MSNBC and Fox News having people who are openly partisan is not the problem. It's ABC, CBS, CNN, NBC, and every mainstream newspaper pretending their anchors and their front page stories are less opinion than Sean Hannity or Rachel Maddow.

For their part, politicians on the left are suppressing their opponents by calling Trump a white supremacist and linking all Republicans to Trump. It doesn't matter that Paul Ryan, Mitch McConnell, and others have clashed with Trump, they are all complicit in his racism. Of course, they don't have any evidence of his racism, but that doesn't matter. In fact, the Left doesn't even know what racism is anymore. This is why a temporary ban on some countries is racist, even though most Muslim majority countries are not included and non-Muslims from the countries included are also banned.

With all of this momentum, they can say anything and it is taken as fact. They say that the tax cuts only help the rich. The numbers prove that is not true but their followers believe it. They say deporting illegal immigrants is racist. Overnight, allowing anyone to stay in the country is the civil rights issue of our time.

Some politicians go beyond challenging policy. Maxine Waters has been yelling, "Impeach 45!" since the beginning of his presidency. Obviously, she had no evidence, there wasn't even an investigation at the time. Now she's upped the ante. She recently called for people to confront and shout down any member of Trump's administration saying, "... tell them they're not welcome anymore, anywhere." [182] She is not alone in her inflammatory rhetoric.

Missouri State Senator Maria Chappelle-Nadal said in a Facebook post, "I hope Trump is assassinated." As of this writing, she is still a state senator. Cory Booker, Kamala Harris, and others have also gone to extreme lengths to attack the president and his administration. Hillary Clinton, who famously called Trump supporters 'deplorables,' has continued her attacks. While speaking in India, Clinton said she won the places that are optimistic, diverse, dynamic, and moving forward. She went on, "You didn't like black people getting rights; you don't like women, you know, getting jobs; you don't want to, you know, see that Indian American succeeding more than you are," implying these are the people who voted for Trump.

On the entertainment front, celebrities have been attacking Trump and his supporters since the campaign. Stephen Colbert was in last place in the late-night race until he made his show a one-stop shop for Trump bashing. Jimmy Kimmel spent months attacking the administration. At least most of his attacks were on policy. He was wrong, but it was a welcomed change to the barrage of personal attacks. Samantha Bee called Ivanka Trump a feckless c**t on live TV, and these are the ones who didn't incite violence.

Madonna famously said she felt like blowing up the White House, one day after the inauguration. Johnny Depp sardonically asked, "When was the last time an actor assassinated a president?" Kathy Griffin posed with Trump's severed head, Snoop Dogg conducted a mock assassination in a video, and Peter Fonda suggested Trump's 12-year old son should be ripped from his mother's arms and put in a cage with pedophiles.

The last group intimidating the opposition is business leaders. Some do it directly, like the GrubHub CEO telling employees to resign if they voted for Trump. Others find indirect ways to do it. When Samantha Bee made the vile comment referenced above, she was working for a cable network. Management could have pulled her show like they did *Roseanne* but chose not to. The same goes for the studio releasing Fonda's movie. Both comments were far more incendiary than Barr's tweet.

When ESPN personalities started to engage in political commentary, no one was there to stop it. Jemele Hill tweeted a racist comment about the president and she was not suspended. Even though Curt Shilling was suspended and subsequently fired for sending far more innocuous tweets. In fact, they recently rehired Keith Olbermann, a man who tweets nasty, profanity-laced tweets at the president regularly. He even wrote a book titled, *Trump Is F*cking Crazy (This is not a joke)*. Only leaders on the Left would allow this behavior.

These actions by the media, politicians, entertainment, and business leaders are proof that the Left is far more oppressive than Donald Trump or anyone on the right can be. Their actions have also created a mob mentality among their acolytes. This mob has been whipped into a frenzy and lack the information or understanding necessary to act rationally. Their attacks are one-sided, and conservatives pay the price.

The mob goes after anyone who doesn't conform to leftist ideology. This results in bad behavior being condoned and people shouting down free speech. The first casualty happens to be college campuses. Years ago, the universities were the base of operations for free speech protection. Now that the Left has taken over the country's educational system, the universities are some of the most intolerant places in the country.

College Republicans need legal assistance and security just to get a conservative speaker accepted at many colleges. But acceptance is only the first hurdle, actually making it through the event is a different story. Conservative speakers are routinely disrespected on college campuses across the country. They are disinvited (Condoleezza Rice), have the events moved (Ann Coulter), are shouted down (Dennis Prager), or booed (Betsy DeVos). These are the successful events. Some result in violence.

When conservative author Charles Murray came to Middlebury College in Vermont to speak, he got more than he expected. He was shouted down and protestors rushed the stage. The professor who invited him was injured. When he couldn't complete the talk, administrators allowed him to finish the talk online. On his way out of the building, he was confronted by angry students donning bandanas to cover their faces.

When Milo Yiannopoulos showed up at UC Berkeley to speak, he was met with protests. The speech was canceled after riots broke out. Antifa, accusing him of being a racist fascist, vandalized the campus and started fires. This is becoming increasingly common. Score one for mob rule.

This divisive climate is worsening the already declining culture. The media continually ran the audio of Trump's infamous Access Hollywood tape. After the election, attendees of the Women's March wore pussy hats. Trump allegedly called some countries "s**tholes" (in private); CNN took the opportunity to say the word many times in its reporting, in spite of the lack of any audio. Respect and decorum have been declining for years, but it has gotten worse with the election of President Trump; he brings out the worst in people.

People now celebrate bad behavior. A congressional intern yelled obscenities at the president and was not terminated. When De Niro opened his presentation at the Tony Awards with f**k Trump, he received a standing ovation. Friendships are ending and family members are cutting each other off over political affiliations. This is a terrible trend and it would be naïve to think things will go back to normal when the president is no longer in office.

Now the divide is so great, the Left doesn't even make consistent arguments. They demand that businesses don't discriminate, while liberal judges rule you can ban people wearing

MAGA hats from your establishment. They argue how hateful and un-American it is for a bakery, who serves gays, to refuse to design a wedding cake for a gay couple. Does this belief extend to coffee shops?

In October of 2017, an anti-abortion group called Abolish Human Abortion was passing out flyers in a Seattle neighborhood. They went into a coffee shop and the owner, who had observed them passing out their flyers, approached them. He demanded that they leave saying, "I have a right to be offended, so I have a right to say get out … Can you tolerate my presence? If I go get my boyfriend right now and f**k him in the ass right here, you're going to tolerate that? Leave, all of you. Tell all of your f**king friends not to f**king come here!"

When one of the group members said, on his way out of the door, "Christ can save you from that lifestyle." Borgman said, "Yeah, I like ass, I'm not going to be saved by anything. I'd f**k Christ in the ass, OK? He's hot!" The video can be found in the endnotes. I chose the post from *Out* magazine because the writer was supportive of the owner; giving him kudos and saying amen to his retort about Christ. As sick as this is, I point to this for consistency. When will the Supreme Court hear the case *Christians who want coffee v. Angry gay shop owner*? The answer is never, because the Christians wouldn't sue and discrimination is fine if done by protected groups.

I remember a time when nearly every business had a sign that stated, "We reserve the right to refuse service." Every business owner had the power, few of them used it. Now people with little time on their hands are suing to take away freedoms. People are suing to force businesses that treated them like crap to serve them.

It's like they're saying, "Judge, please make this guy who hates me give me bad service and use the proceeds to support causes I don't believe in." Why would anyone want to eat food prepared by a cook who wishes he could put you out? In any event, it seems that the Left can refuse to serve anyone while conservatives have to get permission.

One of the strangest cultural shifts is the hatred of men. More specifically white men. It's about as hip a fad as the man bun, and like that fad, it doesn't make sense. These men are our friends, co-workers, and beloved actors and musicians. They are fathers, sons, brothers, pastors, doctors, and chefs. We love them, as individuals. Yet, as a group, they are toxic, vile, immoral, and should die.

It may say something that many of the culprits are academics. It's just another example of universities aiding in the cultural demise. Tommy Curry, an associate professor at Texas A&M wrote, "When is it OK to Kill Whites?" Trinity College Professor Johnny Eric Williams called whites "inhuman a**holes" and said, "Let them die." Recently, Louisville's Ricky Jones asked in an article, "Was James Baldwin right when he called white Americans moral monsters?"

The *New York Times* recently hired Sarah Jeong to their editorial board. She was quickly attacked by conservatives as a racist for many tweets that resurfaced of her making racist, despicable comments. What's interesting is the multiple articles explaining why she's not racist. Among the defenses are, 'she was replying to trolls' and 'she didn't mean them literally.' Aren't these the same things Trump supporters say about him? The difference is, he has never said anything resembling, "oh man it's kind of sick how much joy I get out of being cruel to old white men," or "Are white people genetically predisposed to burn faster in the sun, thus logically being only fit to live underground like groveling goblins?" These things take thought.

In June of 2018, the *Washington Post* ran an op-ed piece by Suzanna Danuta Walters entitled, "Why can't we hate men?" In it, she took some truly awful actions by a small number of men, mixed in some generalities and wrapped all of that in many of the myths we covered in the chapter on gender. For this, she's been lauded as strong and honest. The fact that the article passed editorial review proves that there is an effort to advance this narrative.

Those examples were of blacks and women but white men like to get in on the action too. A Drexel University professor, George Ciccariello-Maher, tweeted on Christmas Eve, "All I want for Christmas is white genocide." Rutgers history professor James Livingston 'resigns' from the white race after run-in with 'Caucasian a**sholes' in Harlem.

The biggest issue with these attacks is not that they are so over the top, or that it shows how angry we've become. It's the number of people who celebrate and defend the comments. It is very telling that people view these professors as credible. If a black man said he wanted all black men to die, people would rightfully, question his mental stability. But since their attacks are directed at white men, people view them as strong men speaking the truth. In fact, they say those who take offense to these comments don't understand race.

Earlier we discussed the lack of free speech on college campuses. There is also a new trend of making totalitarian demands of the administration, faculty, and other students. A group of black students at UC Santa Cruz staged a sit-in. Their demands were to guarantee four years of housing for all black students, to require diversity training for incoming students, and to paint the Rosa Parks African Theme House the colors of the black liberation flag. After three days, the administration agreed to them.

In a perfect lesson for the administrators who capitulate to blackmail, the problem wasn't resolved. Shocked by the victory, the students added three new demands. They now wanted the university to purchase a property to serve as low income housing for historically disadvantaged students, allocate $100,000 for Santa Cruz's "SOMeCA" student organization support department, and create either a Black Studies department or a Black Studies minor or major.

This is now common behavior on campuses. They demand safe spaces and cry rooms. It is now offensive to hear ideas one disagrees with. The grandchildren of those heroes who fought to end segregation are creating segregated graduations. In response, cowardly administrators acquiesce. They remove Shakespeare from the curriculum of English majors, ban whiteboards, and offer full scholarships to refugees.

In 2017, Harvard announced that any male or female student who chooses to join a 'single-gender' club will be penalized. They held off on the push to ban the groups but denounced the existence of these groups as pernicious. To be clear, they are penalizing students for joining fraternities and sororities.

This constant push for diversity and preference has consequences, and when achieving diversity is your primary focus, you miss the fact that it is causing disastrous effects. You may think it's wrong to deport illegals, but the answer should not be favoring them over citizens in need.

In Oregon, a judge helped an illegal immigrant charged with a DUI escape ICE. Oakland Mayor Libby Schaaf warned illegals about an impending ICE raid, several of whom had been convicted of violent felonies. Finally, NYC Governor Andrew Cuomo pardoned seven illegals to prevent them from being deported. Blacks constantly talk about the criminal justice system treating them unfairly. I'd like to ask when was the last time they can recall blacks getting this level of service from government officials?

We discussed the crisis the country faces with its boys earlier. There is a shortage of role models, and it seems we're making the situation worse. Half of them grow up with no male in the house, the schools are treating them like wild horses that need to be broken; now there is a systematic move to get rid of all single-gender organizations. When they're all gone, we'll have a win for diversity but at what cost? If the number of men at home raising boys is decreasing and they can't join any groups to bond with other boys and learn from men, where will this much-needed development come from?

The anti-police crowd wants less policing in minority neighborhoods; this results in more crime. A recent report from Baltimore shows what the consequences of less policing are.[183] After the high profile death of Freddie Gray and its subsequent riots, Baltimore saw first-hand the dire results of the 'Ferguson Effect'. This is the highly disputed argument that in Ferguson, Missouri police relaxed their efforts against crime after the riots that followed Michael Brown's death. Some disputed this argument while others said it was simply too early to tell. Now that three years have gone by since Freddie Gray's death, there is enough data to make a conclusion and the results are glaring.

The USA Today reviewed police records and found that incidents where officers questioned people without being called dropped 70%. As the investigator said, "Police officers reported seeing fewer drug dealers on street corners. They encountered fewer people who had open arrest warrants. Police questioned fewer people on the street. They stopped fewer cars." Donald Norris, an emeritus professor at the University of Maryland Baltimore County, who reviewed *USA TODAY's* analysis added, "The outcome of that change in policing has been a lot more crime in Baltimore, especially murders, and people are getting away with those murders."

Under the guise of inclusiveness, the Left is celebrating gender fluidity. It's one thing to support transgender people, it's another thing to encourage the behavior. Parents are increasingly allowing their children to choose their sex. In some cases, the child says he or she is the opposite sex and they confirm it. In others, they remove all mentions of gender. A recent *NBC News* report followed a new trend of parents who are raising 'theybies': genderless babies.[184] Increasingly, it's the government who is promoting the cultural decline.

In Delaware, the Department of Education will allow children, as young as five, to choose their race and gender, without the consent of the parents.[185] In late 2015, a Texas teacher was fired for not addressing a six-year old girl as a boy, in the middle of the school year.[186] Recently, leftist judges, who follow social trends rather than the law or common sense, place the rights of a biological boy who wants to shower with the girls over the girls who are uncomfortable with it. When in doubt, always side against normative behavior.

Many, like me, have been complaining that children aren't being taught accountability anymore. How can we expect them to learn it when their teachers aren't good examples? The NYC schools implemented a literacy test to measure the competency of their teachers. They decided to scrap the test because they found that a disproportionate number of minority teachers failed it.

This is problematic on many levels. My first concern is that the minority performance was the biggest focus. Does this mean if the white teachers failed too, there would have been no problem? Then there's the fact that they don't understand what it means to measure. The whole point was to find out the competency levels and improve accordingly. You don't scrap a teaching tool because it shows improvement is needed. The worst part is that white teachers only scored 64% on the test, so it seems that few of the teachers are prepared to teach regardless of their race.

Finally, we are no longer able to say any behavior is bad. Recently, a black man was killed by police in Chicago. People immediately protested. News spread that the police had shot another unarmed man. That was quickly proven false. The police released bodycam footage of the man with a gun. The protestors then said he was carrying the gun legally; that too was false. This is where it gets crazy. The protests persisted. His defenders said that they needed to hear the audio because the police may have incited him. Some claim that he may have been 'unaware' he could not legally carry the firearm.

If we allow this behavior to be acceptable now, what will the future hold? We already have racial animus, senseless crime, religious bigotry, class envy, and all of the other time-tested human ills. Now we've added Republicans are Nazis, white men are evil,

Trans is the new black, babies can be genderless, video game addictions, and be rude to people you disagree with. How far will it go if no one says, "Enough"?

People often ask Republicans how they can support Trump. I was a never-Trumper and I have no problem admitting that he has said and done some stupid and indefensible things. In answering that question, some simply like the fact that they have a fighter and they don't care how he does it. For others, they are pleasantly surprised. From a policy standpoint, he's more conservative than George W. Bush. As for his rhetoric, they take him seriously but not literally, while the Left takes him literally but not seriously.

I believe it's good for Trump supporters to question their allegiance. This keeps them honest. But who keeps the Left honest? If I have to question myself whenever I agree with the president, when do liberals and independents have to question themselves? It is time for independents and liberals to ask themselves how long they'll be able to support the Democratic Party.

Elected officials are calling to abolish ICE and encouraging the act of shaming people out of society. Those who call to abolish the police, borders, and profits are no longer on the fringes. Sticking with policy issues, the Left openly defies federal immigration laws and the co-chair of the Democratic Party is calling for a 'Marshall Plan' to build up Mexico's economy. The Democrats are also electing socialists and calling everything racist and treasonous.

You can think Trump is bad and disagree with his policies, but on the bigger issue of culture, there's no question who is doing the most harm. The Left is allowing pre-teens to choose their sex, endorsing pedophilia and infanticide, spreading hatred of whites, and pushing for illegals to vote.

For clarity sake, I would challenge any independent, classic liberal or never-Trumper to make a list of all of the media stories they find that are untrue or misleading, all of the economic policies they disagree with, and all of the cultural changes they think are too extreme, and link them to the Left or the Right. After doing this exercise they will discover that, without question, they associate the vast majority of these things to the Left. With that in mind, we will finish this journey by discussing ways to combat the dangerous agenda the Left is advancing ever so quickly.

· 8 ·

Stemming the Tide

*What a culture we live in, we are swimming in an
ocean of information, and drowning in ignorance.*
— **Richard Paul Evans**

The book to this point has been a detailed explanation of how we got here. We discussed the abundant examples of inequality throughout history: the horrendous social and legal obstacles that blacks and other minorities had to face, the necessary and moral fight many endured to gain equality for groups being discriminated against, and finally the unfortunate push for preference which contradicts the equality they say they want and many actually fought for. The remainder of the book will be about where we go from here.

Obviously, my target audience is not the Left. They are not only happy about the direction the culture is taking, they are pushing for it. But the message is not and should not be construed as a message for conservatives only. There are plenty of independents and liberals who may disagree with conservatives on a lot of policy issues but are not comfortable with where our culture is headed. This message is for anyone who loves America, because the decline has very little to do with policy. Here are some important points we need to understand and focus on to stop the downward spiral and to begin moving our culture back to the center.

THEY WANT SOCIALISM

It is important to understand the Left doesn't want to just tinker with the edges, they want a different country. Up until now, it had been unpopular to say the things they believe and have an audience or run for office, so they kept their true feelings quiet. Conservatives were accused of over-the-top rhetoric for saying that Democrats want to make America a socialist country. Now prominent Democrats are starting to say it publicly.

Today, it is easy to find politicians who advocate reducing the size and scope of law enforcement, raising taxes, giving everyone a mandatory wage, banning all social restrictions, closing jails, free college, free healthcare, and more. Because of the cultural shift, more people than ever before believe that socialism is the answer, however, that number is nowhere near a majority. We need to present the two positions to the people and let them decide. The problem is when they are not honest about what they want, they sound like they just have the country's best interest at heart. You, in turn, sound like you don't want to help people.

Let's be honest, socialism sounds good. Bernie Sanders became a folk hero of sorts espousing the utopia of socialism. In a fair election process, he would have been the Democrat nominee for president in 2016. In his campaign, he advocated for free college tuition, a living wage, social justice, sanctuary cities, and economic equality. In his America, everyone who needs help gets it, the government takes care of everything and it's all free to 99% of us. If the 1% pays their 'fair share,' we can pay for everyone's needs. Except we can't.

Anyone who understands history knows that socialism has never worked. There have been many attempts, but they all ended poorly. If the society which tested socialism was lucky, they only experienced greater poverty and a few failed businesses. In the worst cases, millions died. Many proponents of socialism argue that it hasn't been implemented properly and detractors wrongly use communism as a comparison and communism is different. While this is an over simplified explanation, it is the quickest and most discernable example of the minor difference between the two.

With socialism, those who have more are asked to give to those who have less. It is the epitome of my term negative equality. They don't strive to find ways to raise up the working class, they will achieve equality by bringing the rich, and subsequently the middle class, down to the level of the working class. Communism, is simply involuntary socialism. When those in power ask you to give and you refuse, they come and take what they want by force. Voila, we've graduated to communism.

It will be interesting to see how the SJWs plan to enforce all of these new regulations if people resist. In order to make legislation compulsory, you need a police force but in addition to advocating for socialism, they also want to abolish the police. These two arguments are mutually exclusive.

Look up the history on many immigrants coming to America in the 20th century from Cuba, Poland, Germany, Russia, etc. They were middle class people who had everything taken from them when the Union of Soviet *Socialist* Republics (USSR), the National *Socialist* German Workers' Party (Nazis), and Fidel Castro's

Communist Party of Cuba came to power. All devolved into dictatorships. But the Left believes that we'll be different.

Putting the ruthlessness and strong-arming aside for a moment, we simply don't have the resources to make this work. This is where they think they have me cornered. We are the wealthiest nation in the history of the world and have an abundance of funds at our disposal. This, of course, is true. What they're ignoring is the fact that the wealth in America is owned by individuals and while many are charitable, none give at the levels the Left would need them to in order to make everything free. No problem, the socialists have a solution: pass a law.

Sanders and his ilk want to cap CEO compensation to a percentage of the workers' salaries. It sounds so benevolent that few focus on the insanity of it. You are saying that the *government* should limit how much a person can be compensated working at a company he or she created, in many cases. I have never started a multi-million-dollar business, but I can imagine what level of creativity, sacrifice, and work goes into achieving that dream. The problem is most of us are selfish. We focus singularly on our own well-being. Since we cannot empathize with millionaires, why would we care if the government took more than half of their money?

While working to limit CEO compensation on the one hand, the Democrats are trying to raise entry-level salaries as high as they can. They have organized marches to 'fight for $15' but Sanders and others are subtly demanding a livable wage. They won't say what that wage is, but we know it's not $15 per hour. To summarize, their idea of economic equality is to cut salaries on one end, raise salaries on the opposite end, all while they continue to push for higher taxes.

You may be thinking that in communism, the government controls the means of production. You are correct and this is one of the big reasons it fails. Government doesn't produce anything and is not in a position to control anything. But if you look closely, the government is deeply involved in most corporations. They subsidize industries like farming, solar panels, and electric cars; they bail out private businesses like banks and car manufacturers; they fund government entities run by the states like Medicare and education; and they regulate industries like utilities, airlines, financial institutions, and telecommunications. This gives the government a massive level of control over companies. The politicians in turn are influenced by lobbyists. With all of these regulatory controls, the government is moving closer to controlling businesses, indirectly, even without the open call for socialism. Imagine how successful they'll be when they're open about it.

"Socialist revolution aims at liberating the productive forces. The changeover from individual to socialist, collective ownership in agriculture and handicrafts and from capitalist to socialist ownership in private industry and commerce is bound to bring about a tremendous liberation of the productive forces. Thus the social conditions are being created for a tremendous expansion of industrial and agricultural production." – Mao Zedong. This comes directly from the top of the socialist food chain.

LEARN TO DECODE THEIR LANGUAGE

The Left has accused Republicans of using 'code words' for years. These words, they claim, are intended to be a wink and a nod to the conservative base, letting them know that they are really speaking ill of some minority group. An example of this would be a Republican saying, 'poor people.' This, in the Left's minds, is an obvious reference to black people. This is a giant leap in their own minds and they have no way of proving intent. In most cases, if you replace poor with black it still doesn't make the statement racist. Take the comment, "Poor people need to work more." Even without the 'code word,' this statement is not racist. There is never a direct connection to the implication.

Conversely, the Left frequently operates in this manner, which is probably why they think the Republicans are doing the same. Their approach is less 'code word' and more 'lie by omission.' When addressing a hot button issue, they minimize the scope of change they desire to a palatable amount. They accept this small step knowing that the final goal is a few steps away. If you can get them to talk about what they want, they inevitably get to the truth. Here is a real-life example.

What if there was a constitutionally protected right that politicians made a concerted effort to block? They went to court to stop you from doing it. When they lost and were mandated to allow their constituents to exercise this right, they made it cost prohibitive when possible and limited the places in which the right can be exercised, making it even more difficult for those living in poor urban areas. All of this having a disparate impact on black and Hispanic citizens. Wouldn't people be protesting?

Well, this happened in Chicago and several other cities across the country. The right is gun ownership. Until they were forced to change by a Supreme Court ruling, it was against the law for any citizen of Chicago to own a handgun. After the ruling, government officials slowly came up with a law to allow gun ownership, but it was so restrictive that the courts made them scrap it and create a new one. As of this writing, there are no gun shops or shooting ranges within the city limits, although they've lost another lawsuit pertaining to this. All of this happened in spite of the fact that most on the Left *say* they simply want to ban 'assault rifles' and to have 'sensible' gun control laws. It's ironic how they say they don't want a gun ban, but they constantly suggest we implement the gun policy of Australia which was a gun ban. Classic leftist bait and switch.

With the retiring of Justice Anthony Kennedy, no topic has been debated more than abortion. Many on the left feel that *Roe v. Wade* will be overturned the day after a new Supreme Court justice is nominated. This is obviously extreme and premature, but it does speak to the Left's views on abortion. As with other talking points, most politicians on the Left say they support 'a woman's right to choose.' They often temper their comments by saying that there should be some limits and abortions should be rare; this, while attending rallies in support of people who demand 'abortion on demand.' They say 'late-term' abortion is an inaccurate term and very few people have them. However, how often they happen has nothing to do with whether or not someone thinks they should be legal or are morally acceptable.

During the 2016 presidential campaign, Democratic nominee Hillary Clinton visited *The View*. Co-host Paula Faris was following up on a question Chuck Todd asked on Meet the Press about the rights of an unborn child. Here is that exchange:[187]

Ms. Faris: You said, 'the unborn person doesn't have constitutional rights.' And my question is at what point

204 | we want EQUALITY

does someone have constitutional rights? And are you saying that a child, on its due date, just hours before its delivery still has no constitutional rights?

Mrs. Clinton: Under our law, that is the case. I support Roe v. Wade because I think it is an important—an important statement about the importance of a woman making this most difficult decision with consultation by whom she chooses ... and under the law, and certainly under that decision, that is the way we structure it.

It may be a stretch for conservatives like Ted Cruz to say that Mrs. Clinton *supports* abortion at this stage, but it is a greater leap to suggest that she doesn't think a woman has a right to do it. In order to have an honest debate and settle the issue, the Left should speak about abortion like the Right speaks about guns. This is not what we get with the 'safe, legal, and rare' mantra they give us.

They also claim to support the 1st amendment, but they must not have read the entire thing because one of the rights mentioned in the 1st amendment is the freedom to exercise one's religion. Everywhere we turn, the Left is trying to erode this right as discussed in the earlier chapter on religion. Yet, if you get them in an interview, they will tell you they support a given person's religious rights, then give you a list of exceptions.

GIVE THEM THEIR ARGUMENT

As you've seen, my Logic Board approach is an effective and unique way to debate issues with the Left. This approach is great for two reasons. The first is that it is not antagonistic. There's no need to call them names or tell them they're wrong. This creates a comfortable environment for them to talk. This leads us to advantage number two: they eventually say what they mean. Many politicians and political pundits are masters of communication. They know how to request less and make you believe that is all they want. You have to force them to say what they really mean and arguing won't get you there. This is where their opponents fail. Instead of hearing their ideas and saying, "You liberals are crazy!" it would be better to just probe a little. You'll be surprised what you may learn.

To highlight this, let's look at two examples: gun control and illegal immigration. The beauty here is that there's no debate. You simply ask follow up questions until they reach an impasse. They will either admit their true desire is far more than their initial request or concede that their plan won't work.

In a debate on gun control, the Left will start with the typical 'I don't want to ban guns, I only want sensible gun control' rhetoric. The first step would be to have them define sensible gun control. Because they have little knowledge of the gun purchasing process, most of them will list a combination of controls that are already in place and things that have a trace effect on gun crime, say private owner sales or gun show loopholes. To this you'd ask them how many times have they heard of a shooting and found that the suspect got his gun from a gun show? The likely answer is zero.

Next you ask them to set aside private sales and gun shows for the moment. Everything else they've mentioned is already in place, so you ask, "What else would you do?" Here it gets interesting. They produce a litany of ideas the Left has floated for years: a gun registry, mental illness checks, licenses to purchase bullets, the legal ability to hold gun manufacturers liable for shootings, mandating that guns remain unloaded, and a slew of additional taxes.

While there are serious constitutional and operational issues with many of these proposals, those are topics for an extended discussion. What's important here is that implementing the above proposals is akin to a gun ban. Many people will find it cost prohibitive to own a gun. Some will lose their guns in the registration process. These consequences will disproportionally affect minority gun owners, making the moves racist by the Left's definition.

Those who could afford it would say, 'what's the point' if they have to keep it unloaded. No one wants mentally ill people to have a firearm, but who gets to determine who's mentally ill? Is someone who suffered from mild depression after the loss of a loved one five years ago a security threat? I, for one, don't want some bureaucratic panel deciding when people lose their rights.

All of these potential issues are meaningless, as the manufacturers will be out of business in months if held liable for gun crimes. No insurance company would touch them (the leftist business leaders we discussed earlier are already trying to find ways to decline credit card purchases to gun dealers). With the number of shootings in the country, they wouldn't have to be found guilty. The legal fees from hundreds of wrongful death lawsuits would bankrupt them.

Don't worry, the Left has a plan for the existing stockpile of guns too. They usually start with a voluntary gun buyback program. Ask if they would make it compulsory if most don't volunteer. If they say yes, ask them to explain how the police will take 300 million guns by force. Who will be addressing crime while they are focused on this task?

The argument for illegal immigration baffles those who operate within the parameters of logic. Conservatives may disagree with gun control advocates on effective ways to reduce gun crimes, but we don't think their reason for wanting gun control is illogical. They may downplay the benefits of gun ownership, but we all see the issues faced by criminals with guns. The same doesn't apply to immigration.

There is no benefit to illegal immigration; period. Many of the people who come here illegally are nice and hard-working. This means nothing in respect to the issue. No one has an inherent right to migrate to any country. There is a process in place for those who want to come here, and everyone seeking to enter should follow it. If that process needs to be adjusted, that is for the citizens and their representatives to decide.

Some say illegals do the work Americans don't want to do. That's debatable, but if it is true, then we should seek immigrants to do the work, like employers who create incentives to attract applicants. But this should be initiated by employers in concert with the government, not by people breaking the law. We should also know the criminal history of those coming into the country. You cannot know that when people cross the border without our knowledge. Our government controls the immigration laws and can easily increase the number of people they admit. But we can't be more inviting to those coming through the front door while millions sneak in through the back door. This is lost on the Left.

Like the earlier gun debate, their political stance on illegal immigration does not align with their actions. They say that they are for border control and just want to be compassionate while implementing it. The Republicans lobby for legislation which would accomplish this and the Left calls it racist. Here are some forgotten quotes on illegal immigration from prominent Democrat pundits and politicians:

"Illegal immigration wreaks havoc economically, socially, and culturally; makes a mockery of the rule of law; and is disgraceful just on basic fairness grounds alone." – Glenn Greenwald

"Immigration reduces the wages of domestic workers who compete with immigrants. The fiscal burden of low-wage immigrants is also pretty clear. We'll need to reduce the inflow of low-skill immigrants." – Paul Krugman

"When I see Mexican flags waved at pro-immigration demonstrations, I sometimes feel a flush of patriotic resentment. When I'm forced to use a translator to communicate with the guy fixing my car, I feel a certain frustration." – Barack Obama[188]

"The first of these seven principles is that illegal immigration is wrong; plain and simple. When we use phrases like 'undocumented workers', we convey a message to the American people that their government is not serious about combating illegal immigration, which the American people overwhelmingly oppose." – Sen. Chuck Schumer[189]

"We have to send a clear message: just because your child gets across the border doesn't mean your child gets to stay." – Hillary Clinton[190]

It's important to note that Schumer's 'seven principles' included border control, biometric-based electronic verification for employment, and mandated that all illegals in the country at the time register and submit to a 'rigorous process' of converting to legal status.

If these quotes were from 50 years ago, you could say the commenters evolved. But these comments were all recent. Clinton was specifically talking about the large number of children that came in after Obama announced DACA in 2014. Here again we'd go to the Logic Board:

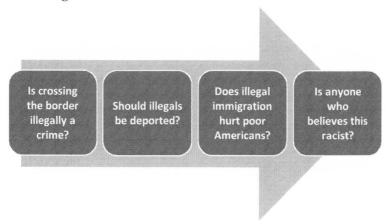

Is crossing the border illegally a crime?

Should illegals be deported?

Does illegal immigration hurt poor Americans?

Is anyone who believes this racist?

If they believe anyone who says these things are invariably racists, then their hero, Barack Obama, and his heir apparent, Hillary Clinton, are both racists. If you point this out, they will likely shift the topic to provocative things Trump has said. You follow with the fact that comments aren't policy and ask what about the policy proposal is racist or unfair. Next, they'll try the 'family separation' policy. You point out the fact that children were detained under Obama, with several being released to human traffickers.[191]

They will likely bring up the many articles calling the Trump administration's accusation that this happened under President Obama false. Here, you can show them the following quote from Jeh Johnson, Homeland Security Secretary under President Obama: "We had 34,000 beds for family detention, only 95 of 34,000 equipped to deal with families. So, we expanded it, I freely admit it was controversial. We believed it was necessary at the time. I still believe it is necessary to remain a certain capability for families. We can't have catch and release, and in my three years we deported, or repatriated, or returned over a million people."[192] Those articles they referenced play into the president's claim of fake news.

The last thing they'll bring up is the wall. Here, I would suggest not defending the wall. Instead, ask if they would be willing to give the Republicans all of the other proposals to reform immigration, if they abandoned the wall. They will undoubtedly say no. Their belief is that people should not be barred from trying to have a better life and people cannot be 'illegal', this at least brings to light what they really believe.

With their true beliefs out in the open, you know there is no way to have a rational debate on the topic. They conflate illegal entry with legal immigration. They say they are not for open borders but won't let the government secure them. When pressed for details, we find that they are against border barriers, deportation of most illegals, holding families in detention centers, or refusing asylum to anyone requesting it.

This process works for any plan the Left proposes. They say there's no difference between men and women; you ask why we need girl-specific programs. They say whites are racist; you ask if that includes Democrats. Whatever the issue, it is better for people to hear them defend their arguments than it is for them to listen to you put them down.

INTERSECTIONALITY

To change the culture, you have to control the language, and the Left is a master of creative wording. Whether it's wacky modifiers like 'social' justice (rather than justice) or 'my' truth (which generally has nothing in common with the truth); switching terminology like 'illegal' becoming 'undocumented,' or 'global warming' becoming 'climate change;' taking over words like 'liberal' or 'feminist;' or redefining words like 'racist' and 'man' and 'woman;' manipulating words is one of the basic weapons in their arsenal. Their latest plot is to change the culture with words that are designed to guilt others into changing their behavior. We've all heard them: trigger warnings, mansplaining, safe spaces, and the latest one: intersectionality.

If the Left loses its battle for the soul of America, it is unlikely it will be because the Right fought back. It is more likely to be destroyed by an internal force; the best candidate for this is intersectionality. Intersectionality is a term used to describe how diverse groups, divided by race, class, gender, religion, etc., are intersected by overlapping discrimination and mistreatment. The goal is to form a united front to fight back against a common enemy; usually the Right or straight white men.

For those of us trying to counter the cultural push, this is our greatest weapon, but few realize it. Since the Right doesn't agree with the premise of intersectionality, they miss the potential it has to create a rift within leftist ideology. It's kind of like the split between the right and moderate wings of the Republican Party, except Republicans are not as vicious with their rivals and don't have a mob. Here's how it works.

Intersectionality is the reason a Muslim group, which includes men who are anti-gay, could protest with a LGBTQ group. If the protest is in support of the BDS movement, a movement demanding sanctions on Israel for its treatment of Palestinians, it makes sense that they unite on this issue. But there's no way this alliance can last. At some point the cultural differences between the secular, nihilistic gays and the religious Muslims will butt heads. Intersectionality demands that one group defers for the sake of the whole. This is unlikely to happen.

This type of clash is currently playing itself out in NYC over admission to specialized public high schools. Mayor Bill De Blasio wants the eight elite high schools to "reflect the city better." He feels the lack of diversity is unfair to black and Latino students as they represent 67% of the city's public-school population but only 10% of the students at these schools. The problem is that the majority of the students are not white, they are Chinese.

In NYC, Chinese students make up 53% of the student body at top-tier schools but are only 6% of the city's population. This discrepancy is because enrollment at these schools is based on test scores and the Chinese kids tend to excel. This is a result of hard work and the structure of their family lives and culture. This, however, upsets the goals of increasing minority enrollment.

To rectify this, the mayor and Schools Chancellor Richard A. Carranza announced a plan in early June to eliminate the exam, in an effort to improve diversity at specialized high schools.[193] There's an obvious problem with minimizing achievement goals and ignoring success. But the bigger problem is how the move creates inequality and animosity among the deserving Chinese students.

Proponents of the mayor's plan claim that the exam is arbitrary, yet arbitrary doesn't mean biased. If the exam consisted of questions that are culturally easier for Chinese student to get correct, then that advantage would be unfair and the arguments against the exam would have merit. This is not the case. To simplify, if the exam tested knowledge of throw pillows and every applicant had an equal opportunity to gain the requisite knowledge, you can't say that it is racially biased.

There must be a reason why Chinese students are doing so well. If the exam isn't about Chinese culture and they aren't getting the answers in advance what can the reason be? They are also outperforming white students.

Those arguing that this is unfair forget that the Chinese students are minorities too. They were discriminated against, prohibited from living in certain areas, banned from entering the country for a period, and paid lower wages. They also looked different and didn't speak the language. What is different? It seems that if you are too successful you can get a racial upgrade. Because of the lower crime rates and higher incomes of the Chinese community, they have become honorary whites.

This is playing itself out at the college level as well. Elite universities like Harvard and Stanford are skipping over highly qualified Chinese students with fantastic grades, impressive extra-curricular activities, and off-the-charts ACT and SAT scores to accept less qualified black and Hispanic applicants. Here are the results of the most recent study of medical school acceptance by race:

US Medical School Acceptance Rates (2013 - 2016) by Race/Ethnic Goup, for MCAT Scores 24-32 and GPAs 3.2-3.8									Averages for Matriculants by Race/Ethnic Group, 2015-2016	
MCAT	24-26	24-26	24-26	27-29	27-29	27-29	30-32	30-32	30-32	MCAT	GPA
GPA	3.20-3.39	3.40-3.59	3.60-3.79	3.20-3.39	3.40-3.59	3.60-3.79	3.20-3.39	3.40-3.59	3.60-3.79		
Asian	5.9%	10.1%	16.6%	14.4%	20.6%	34.9%	27.3%	40.3%	57.5%	32.8	3.73
White	8.0%	14.0%	22.0%	19.0%	29.0%	43.0%	34.0%	48.0%	63.0%	29.2	3.73
Hispanic	30.5%	38.3%	51.1%	42.8%	59.5%	71.6%	57.0%	75.9%	83.4%	31.8	3.59
Black	56.4%	67.1%	74.9%	75.3%	81.2%	86.6%	82.3%	86.9%	93.7%	27.3	3.48
ALL	16.7%	20.2%	26.5%	23.2%	30.6%	42.7%	34.5%	46.5%	60.9%	31.4	3.70

Source: Association of American Medical Colleges

When called on the practice, the schools say that they consider other factors as well to ensure a well-rounded student. In reality, this is intersectionality saying that, because the Left's primary goal is diversity, Chinese students are supposed to take one for the team. It is only a matter of time before some group pushes back and calls these actions what they are; racist.

Earlier this year, Emma Stone got a crash course in intersectionality. At the 90th Academy Awards, Stone was tasked with presenting the nominees for Best Director. In her introduction, Stone said, "These four men, and Greta Gerwig, created their own masterpieces this year." She got caught up in the #MeToo movement. She thought she was hip and woke; then the Left attacked.

The critics swiftly attacked her in magazines, newspaper editorials and on social media. What was her crime? You see, two of those 'men' were minorities. Jordan Peele, one half of the comic duo Key and Peele, is black. Guillermo del Toro is a Mexican filmmaker. Many felt that only saying Gerwig's name minimized their historic accomplishments. April Reign, the creator of #OscarsSoWhite, tweeted, "I'm not here for the participation trophies & partial credit some are so eager to give out. Emma Stone made a movie with Woody Allen, played a whitewashed character, and erased the importance of two men of color in a category. But she identified a woman … yay?" She went on to say, "Intersectionality isn't a thing that many white women do well. Emma Stone (and those applauding her) are prime examples."[194] I guess being black or Hispanic trumps being white on the grievance scale, regardless of gender.

Looking at every group, business, or organization and counting those who are members of a minority group is destined for failure. Not because it is the wrong way to achieve equality, though it is, but because you will never be able to satisfy everyone. Every minority group has an organization fighting on its behalf. CAIR, NAACP, NOW, NCLR (La Raza), and GLAAD all advocate on behave of their chosen group. All say their goal is equality, but how do you achieve equality by fighting solely for gays or women? At some point, an issue will come down to resources or power being allotted to only one group, they will all fight for their own. In the end, intersectionality brings out a stronger strand of the very tribalism they claim Trump invokes.

We are already seeing signs of this. A Loyola Chicago student chided the illegal immigration debate, not because she doesn't support illegals, but because she feels black illegals aren't getting enough attention. Black students at Stoneman Douglas echoed this expressing concern that only the white students were being heard after their school shooting.[195] Soon, everyone says their victimhood one-ups another groups'. Intersectionality will bring the Left more pedagogic exposure than any history lesson could.

RECRUIT LIBERALS AND INDEPENDENTS

Stemming the tide on the cultural decline is not a conservative problem and should not be a conservative fight. Much of the discussion comes back to politics even though the problem is not a political one. That is because legislation is the mechanism used to solidify a given agenda. LGBTQ issues and their promotion are about the culture, but legalizing gay marriage is the government implementation of that cultural promotion. Laws are intended to be our representative's way of governing the people the way they want to be governed. This is why presidential executive orders are so troublesome. This is a one-man mandate, usually because he cannot get the measure passed through Congress. In any event, political action should follow the desires of the culture.

This is why it's important to recruit independents and classical liberals. Most of these people who identify as independents are really disillusioned Democrats and Republicans. I would argue that very few people are actually centrists. Many say they are fiscally conservative but socially liberal. That may be true, but it says nothing of their party affiliation. How they weigh the two is what is important. Most of the people I know fit that description. So why are such a large percentage of them Democrats? Because they weigh their socially liberal traits as far more important than their fiscally conservative ones. This seems bad for conservatives, but you have to dig deeper.

When you take politics out of the equation and ask these 'independents' about specifics, they start to move back to the right. Take my typical black friend in his mid-forties. He says he's a Democrat. He distrusts Republicans and hates Trump. However, ask about the hot button issues of the day or the leftist demands, and he sounds more like Rush Limbaugh than Chris Matthews. He decries high taxes, the transgender movement, and illegal immigration. He thinks work ethic and God are lacking in society today.

He believes that racism is still a problem in America, and buys into the notion that it is fomented by Donald Trump; however, he admits it's not a problem in his everyday life. He thinks Black Lives Matter is well-intentioned but misguided and believes the black community needs to be more introspective. Finally, he believes there's racism within police departments and it needs to be addressed, but he doesn't paint all blacks who were shot by police as innocent victims.

I'm convinced those who are fighting the Left can reach many people like this, if they tried. Most don't even point out the true enemy. The Left is destroying the culture and that should be the biggest concern. This is why I rarely talk about Trump. Whenever I get the opportunity to talk about what's going on today my theme is a take on Bill Clinton's 'It's the economy, stupid!' motto; I say, "It's the culture, stupid!"

When someone does bring up Trump, I hold a mirror up to society. They ask if I heard the latest about Trump and I say, "No. Have you seen the videos of parents recording their kids saying vile things and posting them on the internet?" They bring him up again and I ask, "Have you seen the woman who made a music video celebrating being on Section 8?" I continue, "What about the professor who says you should be able to legally kill your infant?"[196] No matter how many times they bring up Trump, I have an endless supply of these far more damaging examples.

Those of us who disagree with the extreme movement to the left need to form a group. Just like the Left is organized, we need to galvanize, then seek out others who see the dangers. An Evergreen College professor refuses to leave the campus when minority students demand that whites do so; sign him up. A University of Chicago professor faces protests for inviting Steve Bannon to speak to students; encourage him. Gay men see problems with linking them to transgender people and the gender fluidity movement; tell them their voices are needed.

The goal here should be to start a movement independent of political views. Anyone who is willing to acknowledge that the Left is killing free speech and hurting the culture is welcome. There must be millions of people in the country who fit these criteria, the problem is people are clinging closely to ideological camps, and the media only invites partisan guests to speak who are willing to tow the party line. If most people felt this way, Donald Trump would not be president.

Working with independents and liberals would be a big step, but none of this works without the never-Trumpers. I understand that if they haven't changed their tune on President Trump in two years, they never will. However, they have to be rational and stop being petty for the good of the country. Let's assume they are correct about Donald Trump. It makes sense, then, to speak out about how bad he is. Where the never-Trumpers go wrong is they fall for the Left's trick. They buy into the 'Trump is evil so anything goes' mentality. There are two examples of this. The first is many of them never have anything good to say about Trump. Even the most ardent critic of the president, if conservative, can find something they like about his policies or his administrative picks; they can find none. The second is they tell people to vote for Democrats. This is telling, since the president is not on the ballot this fall.

So, to them, every Republican is Trump. This also means they are willing to overlook all of the wacky propositions the Left is advancing. I don't think I'm asking too much to have conservative Trump haters stop promoting Democrats and point out the troubles the country faces if the culture continues to decline. Their voices would carry extra weight, since no one can accuse them of defending Trump and their anti-Trump stance makes them the only venerated Republicans in the country.

PUSH BACK

This new strand of leftism is aggressive. When I was in my twenties, they were methodical in their movements. They did affirmative but subtle things to advance their agenda. Now that their foundation has solidified, they are ready for an all-out assault on what's left of traditional norms. It's as if they are sleeper cells and have been activated. It seems like yesterday the country was debating whether same-sex marriage should be the law of the land. Since then, we've moved so far so fast, it's shocking that was even considered debatable.

We've seen a president blackmail schools into allowing transgender students to use the bathroom of their choice; boys competing in girls' sports, beating them handily; parents and schools allowing elementary school students to pick their gender; and a movie where a woman has sex with a sea creature win best picture. I think it's safe to say that traditional Americans have let go of the rope in this crucial game of tug-of-war.

The situation is pretty grim, but it's not too late to make a change. The first step is the most obvious one, push back. The Left must face some resistance. To some, silence is acceptance. When the socialists say they want to abolish the police, you can't just roll your eyes and keep moving. People need to say just how foolish that is. We can't expect the media to do it. Has anyone asked Ocasio-Cortez, if we abolish borders, prison, and the police, then ban guns, who is going to protect us from the newly released prisoners, brandishing illegal guns, after the Left tears down the criminal justice system?

This is one thing we have going for us; the Left is awful. They are so extreme, bitter, vile, judgmental, and often violent that most people who aren't on the left has to view them with opprobrium. It's important to point out how they operate without getting dragged down in the mire with them. We would simply expose the Left for the fascistic tactics they use, evidenced by the myriad examples they provide us on a daily basis.

When people are attacked by the mob, they need to fight back. Don't apologize if you don't think you did anything wrong. Those attacking you won't believe you anyway. Just once I'd like to see a comedian, under fire for an insensitive joke, say, "It was a joke, get over it. Hey, at least I didn't suggest that people die."

Let me be clear, we should not be asking that Bill Maher, Michelle Wolf, John Oliver, or Joy Behar be fired, we should just demand consistency. Either everyone can make hateful comments on air, or no one can.

Some of these employers need to get spines as well. It seems like the only leaders who stand by their employees in a crisis are leftist. The *New York Times* is standing by Sarah Jeong, UC Fresno stood by the professor who said she was glad Barbara Bush was dead, and MSNBC is standing behind Joy Reid, in spite of her lying about her hateful comments. But Kevin Williamson, James Demore, and Hank Williams, Jr. didn't get the same protection from *the Atlantic*, Google, and the NFL respectively.

We don't need to stage a boycott every time someone makes a comment we don't like, but when companies let us know they don't want business from people like us, we should oblige them. We can also counter this by going out of our way, when possible, to support businesses that share our values. This is a positive move rather than the typical anger from the Left.

Next, it's important to engage everyone you can. This doesn't mean getting into shouting matches with family or debates with strangers at the dry cleaners, it simply means finding out what average people think about the issues in the news by asking probing questions. When I'm in a business and something political comes on, I just say, "Crazy, huh?" to see if they'll bite. You'll be surprised where the conversations may go.

I do this everywhere I go. I discuss issues at work, with family, at concerts, dinner parties, you name it. Once you engage, you have to know your stuff. When you speak to people from all walks of life, you never know what their views will be. You are bound to come in contact with someone who only knows leftist talking point. They've never heard an alternative view, so you have one chance to make an impact. No pressure.

I usually give them enough to make them question what they've been told without trying to shatter their views in one conversation. If, for instance the conversation lead to socialist things: free healthcare, tuition etc. I say something like this, "I can see why you'd find that appealing. Keep in mind that governments are run by people and if you give them too much control, they will eventually do things that you don't like. What will you do then when you've relinquished so much power?" Then I give them a couple examples from the country leftists most want us to emulate: Denmark.

I tell them to Google Denmark's plan to eradicate immigrant 'ghettos' and force them to learn 'Danish Values.'[197] I then say,

"They also have a veil ban, blasphemy laws, an official language, and an official religion.[198] Look that up too, I wouldn't want you to take my word for it. That is how I end the conversation. If I see them again, I follow up, otherwise, I hope that I gave them enough to make them reconsider granting too much power to the government.

Some may not be willing to engage strangers in political conversations, especially in this climate. There are other steps you can take. You should contact your representative, especially if he is a leftist. They get lost in their own beliefs, someone has to let them know that the people they represent don't necessarily agree with them. They are also always campaigning. If you can solicit enough support for an idea, fear of losing an election would force him to pay attention.

You could donate to causes that are doing the fighting for you. There are many groups pushing back on many fronts: leftist college ideology, educating young conservatives, defending those attacked by the Left, etc. Find one and donate cash. Seek out those who think like you. You'd be surprised how many logical people there are out there, even in liberal bastions like Chicago.

Using the tactics in this chapter is the catalyst to turning the tide on our culture. It is not going to be easy or a quick fix, but the first step must be taken. We need to be vigilant, keeping the steps concise. Get them to state their actual goals; give them their argument; educate people; push back when attacked; repeat.

If we do this everywhere we can, people will listen. When you get discouraged, look at the Left. They started with subtle moves, quietly chipping away at the traditional norms. They lost a lot of battles but kept moving. Now they are dominating every sector of the culture. Why can't we do the same to build the country up rather than tear it down?

I've given a lot of information about the direction of our culture and its negative impact. It was important to thoroughly explain the problems, give clear examples, and describe what the problems will lead to if we allow the decline to continue. I'm hoping this will reinforce some things the reader knew and teach them some new details they can use to debate those still living in the dark. I understand it is natural for people to take a passive role. I hope that through these examples they realize that the majority of the Left's success in the cultural shift can be attributed to the fact that we sat idly by as it happened.

I'd love for everyone who reads this book to use it as a guide for dealing with the Left in a new and direct way. I know I said a lot here, so I'd like everyone to take two things from this book. (1) Human nature is flawed and while we should fight our negative nature, this is not something that can be fixed with new laws or a new type of government. (2) Think about true equality. Any plan that gives one group preference over another should be instantly dismissed. Keep in mind that it's not a right or equality if someone else has to give something up for you to have it.

Afterword

Information moves incredibly fast. One of the most difficult aspects of writing this book was maintaining focus with so much in the news that is relevant to the topic. In the final months, as I was completing this book, I tried to cut myself off from any news reports, or at least not consider them. This was extremely difficult as many would have fit perfectly into the book. A few even made it in. But I desperately needed to maintain my goal, which was to paint a broad picture of the cultural change. I needed to make it evident that the cultural shift to the Left did not start in 2016. Therefore, the references could not be too heavily weighted to the last year and a half.

In writing a book that is predicated on your opinion, you need to do a strong job of backing up your points. Examples are key. This leads to a lot of research. What I found is that researching history, while tedious, is nothing compared to finding examples of behavior in the media and pop culture. Not because there aren't enough, but because there are too many. My memory was tested often during this process. In many cases, I wanted to tell a specific story I recalled, but I had forgotten some of the details. Because of this, I did a lot of 'Guy in a city who said that thing to an Asian woman' type of searches.

I also didn't want to be viewed as living in an echo chamber, using skewed data from sources favorable to conservatives. I, therefore, tried to avoid conservative sources as much as possible. You will see no references to Breitbart, the Blaze, Drudge Report, or talk radio. If I used them, it's only because I had a specific story to tell and the liberal outlets didn't run it or there was a specific quote or interview I wanted to reference. Of the 211 endnotes, there are only two such examples (In full disclosure, there is one more in this section referencing George W. Bush).

For instance, in the chapter on income, I pointed out that there are tens of thousands of jobs currently going unfilled, with no college degree required, that pay more than the $15 an hour the Left is demanding. Mike Rowe did an interview that was a perfect illustration of what I was describing. He did the interview on *Tucker Carlson Tonight*, so I had to reference *Fox News*. Most of the stories I reference, however, come from the *New York Times*, the *Guardian*, *CNN*, and the *Washington Post*, hardly right-wing publications.

There are obviously many talented conservatives with TV programs, radio shows, magazines, and podcasts. This means I left out many examples that perfectly align with my arguments, because of the source. This left me reliant upon stories delivered with a liberal slant. The media bias that conservatives speak about is not only evident in the dubious ways in which they cover national news stories, it is glaring in the stories they don't cover.

Take gun control as an example. Most of the mainstream media support increased gun control measures. Because of this, they rarely report cases of criminals being stopped or women protecting themselves through legal gun possession. These stories don't help their cause so they are largely ignored. There are many stories like this that would have strengthened my points, but I didn't use them because they are mostly reported in conservative outlets. Fortunately, though left-leaning, many outlets still ran pieces with journalistic integrity, at least they did prior to Trump's election.

As I noted above, I tried to steer clear of Donald Trump for as long as I could. Because my focus is the culture, giving too much attention to attacks on Trump or spending too much time defending him, would have taken away from the important message of the book. It is, however, important to make it clear that neither the country's problems nor the attacks on conservatives are truly about Donald Trump. He simply makes himself an easy target both by his manner of speaking or unorthodox ways and by attacking the Left; they've never seen that before.

The vitriol against Trump is so bad that people conveniently forget how Republican presidents, or candidates for president, have been treated by the Left. Mitt Romney, John McCain, and George W. Bush are nearly folk heroes on the Left today. Look at all of the positive press they've gotten since Trump announced his presidential run. Being a conservative who speaks out against Trump apparently absolves all past sins. But let's take a look back.

When Mitt Romney was the 2012 Republican presidential nominee, he wasn't taken as seriously as he is when he's bashing Trump. Instead he was a wealthy plutocrat who liked firing poor people.[199] In fact, he was a sexist (for carrying around 'binders full of women'),[200] a purveyor of animal cruelty (for forcing a dog to ride on top of a car),[201] a homophobe (for allegedly having bullied a gay teen back in high school),[202] and a murderer (for being the cause of a woman's death with his evil corporate takeovers).[203] They even mocked him for his crazy belief that Russia was a threat to the US.

George W. Bush is no longer the Rodney Dangerfield of politics. One thinly veiled attack on President Trump and he's the toast of the town. Liberals joyously quote him and celebrate his return to

228 | we want **EQUALITY**

the media spotlight ... Glenn Greenwald called him "a good man," while Jedd Legum, the editor of *ThinkProgress*, asked, "When did George W. Bush become the voice of reason?"[204] This is a far cry from their old tune.

In 2005, Glenn Greenwald said, "George W. Bush is a pillaging, torturing war criminal who let a city drown." He was not alone. People chanted 'Bush lied, people died' nearly his entire presidency. He was also a racist and stupid. Remember, Ivy League degrees only mean you're smart if you're on the Left. There was even a TV show on Comedy Central that mocked him, *That's My Bush!*, and a movie that recounted the events leading up to his fictional assassination, *Death of a President*. Some even compared him to, wait for it, Hitler.[205]

John McCain has gotten mixed results from the Left. They are as schizophrenic toward him as his policy decisions have been within Republican ranks. He is an honest politician when reaching across the aisle (McCain-Feingold), and a right-wing extremist when working with the Republicans. As far as attacks from the Left, he faired far better than both Romney and Bush. He was just mentally unstable, misogynistic (allegedly called his wife a c**t in public), racist (supported the Confederate flag and voted against MLK Day), and a war monger (changed the words of the Beach Boys song Barbara Ann to Bomb Iran).[206] If that wasn't enough, he was out of touch, had cancer four times, and would die in office.[207] His supporters, like Trump's, were also racists.[208]

These are examples that, though Trump is different, the labeling of Republicans is not. To codify my argument that the two sides don't act the same, people are punching Trump supporters, putting them out of restaurants, trying to run them over because they have

MAGA bumper stickers, and snatching hats from them. Did these things happen to Obama supporters when he was president?

All of this ties into the cultural issues America faces. When discussing demands for equality, one cannot ignore cultural norms and societal behaviors. These things play a dramatic part in how people perceive they are being treated as well as what determines their idea of equality. Many know Richard Carlson's famous book, *Don't Sweat the Small Stuff, and It's All Small Stuff*. I often joke that I live by an alternate version of this, "Only sweat the small stuff." I'm only half joking, as I believe the small stuff leads to the big stuff. A thief doesn't start a life of crime by breaking into Fort Knox. A drug dealer doesn't start a drug empire by purchasing directly from the head of a Cartel. The same holds for bad behavior. Before we get to intolerance, violence, or discrimination, there are small actions that act as indicators.

I like to monitor behavior. It's fascinating to see how nice the average person can be, at times, and rude and selfish at other times. In this climate, the Right, myself included, likes to point out the nastiness of the Left with regard to reactions they have against varying political views; however, I notice this behavior in smaller arenas with people across the political spectrum.

You can no longer get off of a train or elevator without someone nearly running you over to get on. The same goes for driving in rush hour traffic. When there is a long line to merge, several drivers will inevitably drive to the front of the line and force their way in. I see this and wonder, what do these people do when they aren't driving? This behavior says something about their character.

Let's look at another example, breastfeeding. Women have been doing it for years with no issue. All of a sudden, it became a civil rights issue. Women demanded dedicated places to breastfeed. Then, even this wasn't enough. They needed to be able to breastfeed, in public, with exposed breasts, *and* people, especially men, were not allowed to look at them. Because we no longer judge behavior, people remained silent. Recently, a runway model walked the runway at a show while breastfeeding her child.[209] This is a direct result of the Left pushing the envelope and the rest of us saying nothing about it.

When I tell people my theory, some compare it to New York's old 'broken windows' policing. This is different because I'm not advocating for police to get involved. I believe it's bad that so many of us know right from wrong but have been programmed to 'not judge' regardless of the circumstances. There are only two things that can prohibit bad behavior, self-control and societal pressures. As we lose God in our lives and parents no longer teach constraint, we have fewer people who can maintain control of their behavior. Couple that with our current culture, which celebrates being different, with no behavioral norms, and makes it verboten to correct any behavior, and things are bound to get worse.

Even if the Left is right about the inequality they seek to correct, they lack focus. Following my approach of giving them their argument, I believe the Left, worse than being wrong, have a problem focusing on issues. Time after time, they complain about a perceived problem but their actions do nothing about it. They say that racism is a big problem. As Elizabeth Warren says, "the hard truth about our criminal justice system: It's racist ... front to back."[210] Why then, would you focus on the racists? You can't force them to change their beliefs. The focus should be on behaviors and criminal acts that blacks engage in as much as it is on the number of black men arrested and how long their sentences are. They only focus on the latter. This does nothing to minimize the arrests.

They say many people are raising families on minimum wage and that is not enough on which to survive. They should focus on getting people marketable skills and teaching work ethic rather than trying to get more pay for jobs that will never be a career or may be automated soon. No matter how evil one may believe corporations are, there's no way they would have so many job openings and continue to offer incentives to get people to apply if the people making minimum wage were qualified and lining up for the jobs.

In my chapter on gender inequality, I focused on how boys are treated because foundation is important and boys cannot push back. But men are also being 'fixed' in media, politics, business, and in society at large. In addition to focusing on having a disproportionate number of LGBTQ characters, heterosexual men are being pushed to be less masculine, metrosexual, and third-wave feminists.

In discussing diversity, I mentioned that Code Black had a Hispanic man playing the head nurse of the ER. What I did not mention is that the character is called 'mamma.' Bonobos, an online men's clothing site, recently aired a commercial called 'evolve the definition.' In it, men of all different ages, colors and looks, read the definition of masculine. They describe how the definition is too narrow and needs to be changed. They go on to say what it means to them. Most just say words with no meaning, one man says, "Being a man means being honest." This makes no sense but for businesses run by the Left, having the right social message is more important than their product.[211]

Lastly, if the goal of gender equality is to truly improve the status of women, this should be done by improving women not tearing down men, or turning them into pseudo women. I believe the question needs to be asked, "If the Left succeeds in decreasing masculinity, who will do the things only masculine men are doing now?"

As we've seen, what we allow to become the norm will affect the way people interact, the policies we enact and our quality of life. More importantly, it does not just affect what we do today. It is the single most important thing that will determine what the country will be for future generations, and it's a factor we can control.

We Want Equality is the operational manual needed to maneuver through the barrage of political, social, and pop culture arguments and to develop logical and effective ways to reject flawed arguments without being antagonistic or condescending. It answers tough questions and will change the equality argument of anyone who approaches it with an open mind.

Acknowledgements

This book is an amalgamation of my reaction to the political discourse and the many conversations I've had about current events. While the topic can be interesting, it may not be as interesting to hear me constantly yammer on about it. I'd like to thank all of the friends and co-workers who put up with me and added to the conversation. Jeanne, Chavis, Ari, Nana, Lynn, Melanie, Jeff, Peter, Joe, and the United Nations team at Mike's Barber Shop, your contributions live throughout these pages.

I am indebted to the team of people who helped me make it to the finish line. Juan Padron and Sandeep Likhar helped me convert my random thoughts to a cohesive message, making a novice seem like a professional. I also want to thank Beata and Mario from Lucky Charm Café for allowing me to occupy space to write for the cost of a cup of coffee.

I owe a particular debt of gratitude to the many people I encountered during the two years I worked on this book. Those honest reactions to questions about sensitive subjects in the oddest places challenged me and helped me hone my responses.

Thank you is never really enough to convey how integral my wife was to the process. She had to assume the role of nearly everyone I thanked above, which is a lot to ask. She was also able to temper her input when her views differed from mine and sacrifice our time so I could write. I am truly blessed to have her.

Finally, I want to thank my son for giving me space to write. If you find any typos or things that don't make sense, those would be the times he decided I was working too much and hijacked my computer. Because of the direction things are going, I don't know what type of country we will leave for his generation. I want to prepare him for the future, whatever it holds. Much of what I do is for him.

Notes

[1] New International Version.

[2] Charles A. Frazee, *World History Volume 1*, (Barron's Educational Series, 1999), pp. 25-28.

[3] Bruce Wetterau, *World History: A Dictionary of Important People, Places, and Events, From Ancient Times to the Present*, (Henry Holt & Co,1994), pp. 16-17.

[4] Ibid., p. 19.

[5] Chester G. Starr, *A History of the Ancient World*, (Oxford University Press, 1991), pp. 123-134.

[6] Neil Kagan, *Concise History of the World: An Illustrated Time Line*, (National Geographic, 2013), pp. 33-60.

[7] Chester G. Starr, *A History of the Ancient World*, (Oxford University Press, 1991), pp. 287-292.

[8] Ibid., pp. 340-348.

[9] Robin Waterfield, *Dividing the Spoils - The War for Alexander the Great's Empire* (hardback), (New York: Oxford University Press, 2011), pp. 273.

[10] Chester G. Starr, *A History of the Ancient World, Second Edition.* (Oxford University Press, 1974), pp. 670-678.

[11] Geoff Emberling, *Nubia: Ancient Kingdoms of Africa.* (Princeton: Princeton University Press, 2011), pp. 9-11.

[12] Jan Vansina, *A Comparison of African Kingdoms*, (Africa, 32(4), 1962), pp. 324-35.

[13] Herodotus, *The Histories,* (London: Penguin Books, 1996), pp. 106-107, 133-134.

[14] Hayim Tadmor. *The Inscriptions of Tiglath-Pileser III, King of Assyria,* (Winona Lake: Eisenbrauns, 2011), p. 29.

[15] Elizabeth Pollard, *Worlds Together Worlds Apart*, (Chicago: W.W. Norton & Company, 2015), p. 249.

[16] Raymond A. Mauny, *The Question of Ghana*, (Africa, 1954), pp. 68-80.

[17] Roger B. Beck, *The History of South Africa*, (New Haven: Yale University Press, 2000), pp. 60-63.

[18] Leonard Thompson, *A History of South Africa*, (New Haven: Yale University Press, 2000), p. 85.

[19] Franz Michael, *China Through the Ages: History of a Civilization*, (Routledge, 1986), pp. 134-145.

[20] Ibid., p. 20.

[21] Arthur Waldon, "The Problem of The Great Wall of China." *Harvard Journal of Asiatic Studies*, (Harvard-Yenching Institute, 43 (2), 1983), pp. 643-663.

[22] Jann Einfeld, *The History of Nations: India*, 2003, pp. 69-75.

[23] Michael Grant, *The Civilizations of Europe*, 1965, pp. 7-17.

[24] Time Frame, *Empires Besieged, TimeFrame AD 200-600*, 1988, pp. 8-17.

[25] Edward Gibbons, J.B. Bury (1974). *The Decline and Fall of the Roman Empire*. AMS Press.

[26] Time Frame, *Fury of the Northmen: TimeFrame AD 800-1000*, 1988, pp. 9-40.

[27] Time Frame, *Barbarian Tides: TimeFrame 1500-600 BC*, 1987, pp. 149-167.

[28] Charles A. Frazee, *World History Volume 1*, (Barron's Educational Series, 1999), p. 25-28.

[29] Lynn Foster, *Handbook to Life in the Ancient Maya World*, (New York: Oxford University Press, 2002), pp. 143-144.

[30] Michel R. Oudijk, *Indian Conquistadors*, (Norman: University of Oklahoma Press, 2007), p. 32.

[31] Arthur A. Demarest and Geoffrey W. Conrad, *Religion and Empire: The Dynamics of Aztec and Inca Expansionism*. (Cambridge, UK: Cambridge University Press, 1984), pp. 57-59.

[32] Stephen C. Schlesinger, *Act of Creation: The Founding of the United Nations: A Story of Super Powers, Secret Agents, Wartime Allies and Enemies, and Their Quest for a Peaceful World*. (Boulder, Colorado: Westview Press, 2003).

33 Yosaburō Takekoshi, *Japanese rule in Formosa*, (London, New York, Bombay and Calcutta: Longmans, Green, and co. 2003).

34 "Unlawful Killings and Enforced Disappearances" (PDF). *Final Report of the Commission for Reception, Truth and Reconciliation in East Timor (CAVR)*. p. 6.

35 Gregory F. Gause, III, *The International Politics of the Persian Gulf*, (Cambridge University Press, 2010); Louise Fawcett, *International Relations of the Middle East*, (Oxford: The University Press, 2013), pp. 263–274.

36 Agence France Presse, "Putin describes secret operation to seize Crimea", *yahoo.com*, https://www.yahoo.com/news/putin-describes-secret-operation-seize-crimea-212858356.html,(Accessed December 17, 2017).

37 Graeme Wood. "What ISIS Really Wants" *the Atlantic*, https://www.theatlantic.com/magazine/archive/2015/03/what-isis-really-wants/384980/, (Accessed December 17, 2017).

38 See https://www.history.com/topics/exploration/christopher-columbus.

39 John Merson, *The Genius That Was China: East and West in the Making of the Modern World*, (Woodstock, New York: The Overlook Press, 1990), p. 72.

40 Philip D. Curtin, *Cross-Cultural Trade in World History*, (Cambridge: Cambridge University Press, 1984), p. 5.

41 Greta Weber, "Shipwreck shines light on historic shift in slave trade," *National Geographic Society*, June 8, 2015, https://news.nationalgeographic.com/2015/06/150605-shipwreck-slave-trade-south-africa-18th-century-brazil/, (Accessed December 17, 2017).

42 Ronald Robinson and John Gallahger and Alice Denny, *Africa and the Victorians*, (London, 1961) p. 175.

43 See https://www.reference.com/history/names-three-major-colonial-powers-7bf565cd9fbc5300#.

44 The Economist, "How to stop the fighting, sometimes," *The Economist*, November 9, 2013

https://www.economist.com/briefing/2013/11/10/how-to-stop-the-fighting-sometimes.

[45] Roland Oliver, *Africa in the Iron Age*, (Cambridge: Cambridge University Press, 1975), p. 192.

[46] David P. Forsythe, *Encyclopedia of Human Rights, Volume 1*, (Oxford University Press, 2009), p. 399.

[47] Barbara Krauthamer, *Black Slaves, Indian Masters: Slavery, Emancipation and Citizenship in the Native American South*, (Chapel Hill: The University of North Carolina Press, 2013), pp. 17–19.

[48] Joann Anderson. "Obama Administration Pays $492 Million to Settle With Indian Tribes — But Ignores Claims of Black Indian Families." *BlackNews.com*, www.blacknews.com/news/obama-administration-pays-492-million-settlement-indian-tribes-ignores-black-indian-families-claims/#.W1-5RvZFxMs (Accessed December 17, 2017).

[49] www.endslaverynow.org/.

[50] Ben Kiernan, *The First Genocide: Carthage, 146 BC*, (Diogenes, 2004), pp. 27–39.

[51] Robert B. Strassler, *The Landmark Thucydides*, (New York: Touchstone Books, 2008), p. 357.

[52] James Marson, "Ukraine's forgotten famine," *The Guardian*, November 18, 2009, https://www.theguardian.com/commentisfree/2009/nov/18/ukraine-famine-russia-holodomor, (Accessed January 4, 2018).

[53] Adam Jones, *Genocide: A Comprehensive Introduction*, (Taylor & Francis, 2010), pp. 171-72.

[54] Karl D. Jackson, *Cambodia, 1975-1978: Rendezvous with Death*. (Princeton University Press, 1992), p. 219.

[55] BBC. "Rwanda: How the genocide happened," *bbc.com*, https://www.bbc.com/news/world-africa-13431486, (Accessed January 4, 2018).

56 Richard Sisson and Leo E. Rose, *War and Secession: Pakistan, India, and the Creation of Bangladesh,* (University of California Press, 1991), p. 306.

57 Will Worley, "Burma: Rohingya children 'beheaded and burned alive' as refugees continue to flood into Bangladesh to escape violence," *The Independent,* https://www.independent.co.uk/news/world/asia/rohingya-burma-myanmar-children-beheaded-burned-alive-refugees-bangladesh-a7926521.html, (Accessed September 20, 2017).

58 Ingebjorg Karstad, "Fleeing DRC to Uganda: Africa's other refugee crisis," *Aljazeera,* https://www.aljazeera.com/indepth/inpictures/fleeing-drc-uganda-africa-refugee-crisis-180301084715204.html.

59 Karin Badt. "Torture in North Korea: Concentration Camps in the Spotlight," *The Huffington Post,* https://www.huffingtonpost.com/karin-badt/torture-in-north-korea-co_b_545254.html.

60 Bethan McKernan, "Syria civil war: More than 320,000 people flee fighting in Deraa in 'largest displacement yet,'" *the Independent,* https://www.independent.co.uk/news/world/middle-east/syria-civil-war-deraa-refugees-evacuation-assad-regime-rebel-fighting-israel-jordan-a8434706.html.

61 Patricia Gossman, "Dispatches: Why Afghans are Leaving," *hrw.org,* https://www.hrw.org/news/2015/09/16/dispatches-why-afghans-are-leaving.

62 Nick Cumming-Bruce. "Over One Million South Sudanese Flee From Violence to Uganda," *nytimes.com,* August 17, 2017, https://www.nytimes.com/2017/08/17/world/africa/south-sudan-refugees-uganda.html.

63 Rocio Cara Labrador and Danielle Renwick, "Central America's Violent Northern Triangle," *cfr.org,* https://www.nytimes.com/2017/08/17/world/africa/south-sudan-refugees-uganda.html.

[64] Joe Parkin Daniels and María Ramírez. "Life's a struggle as Venezuela inflation heads for one million percent," *theguardian.com*, July 25, 2018. https://www.theguardian.com/world/2018/jul/25/venezuela-inflation-crisis-nicolas-maduro.

[65] Jeff Hay, *The Early Middle Ages, Turning Points in World History,* (Greenhaven Press, 2001), pp. 157–163.

[66] David E. Guinn, *Protecting Jerusalem's Holy Sites: A Strategy for Negotiating a Sacred Peace*, (Cambridge University Press, 2006), p. 142.

[67] Thomas A. Idinopulos, *Jerusalem blessed, Jerusalem cursed*, (Lanham: Rowman & Littlefield, 1991), p. 152.

[68] Desmond Stewart, *Early Islam*, (Time, 1967), pp. 52–65.

[69] Edward Peters, *The First Crusade*, (Philadelphia: University of Pennsylvania Press, 1971).

[70] F.S. Northedge, *The League of Nations: It's Life and Times, 1920-1946*, (New York: Holmes & Meier, 1986), pp.192-193.

[71] Edward Peters, *Inquisition*, (Berkeley: University of California Press, 1989), p. 54.

[72] H.H. Ben-Sasson, *A History of the Jewish People*, (Cambridge: Harvard Free Press, 1976), pp. 588–590.

[73] Anwar G. Chejne, *Islam and the West, the Moriscos: A Cultural and Social History*, (Albany: SUNY Press, 1983), p. 1-16.

[74] Christopher Snedden, *Kashmir: The Unwritten History*, (India: HarperCollins, 2013), p. 56.

[75] Orla Guerin, "Egypt Christians living in fear for the future," *BBC News*, April 27, 2017, https://www.bbc.com/news/world-middle-east-39694408, (Accessed May 21, 2018).

[76] Eliza Griswold, "Is This the End of Christianity in the Middle East?" *The New York Times*, https://www.nytimes.com/2015/07/26/magazine/is-this-the-end-of-christianity-in-the-middle-east.html?_r=0 (Accessed May 21, 2018).

77 Franz Michael, *China Through the Ages: History of a Civilization*, (Routledge,1986), p. 237.

78 Harriet Sherwood, "More than 20% of countries have official state religions – survey," *The Guardian*, October 3, 2017, https://www.theguardian.com/world/2017/oct/03/more-than-20-percent-countries-have-official-state-religions-pew-survey.

79 AAP, "PNG police arrest 29 alleged cannibal cult members," *News.com.au*, https://www.news.com.au/world/cannibal-cult-members-nabbed-in-png/news-story/471de55a758b19f83d3db6803426d749, (Accessed May 22, 2018).

80 Michael Rudolph. (2008). Ritual Performances as Authenticating Practices. LIT Verlag Munster. p. 78.

81 William Napier, *History of General Sir Charles Napier's Administration of Scinde,* (London: Chapman and Hall, 1851), p. 35.

82 Martti Nissinen, *Homoeroticism in the Biblical World: A Historical Perspective,* (Augsburg Fortress, 1998), p. 57.

83 See CDC Website.

84 See US Holocaust Memorial Museum.

85 Yuki Tanaka. *Hidden Horrors,* (Westview Press, 1996), p.138.

86 Boris Volodarsky. *The KGB's Poison Factory,* (Zenith Press, 2009), p. 34.

87 Ana Simo. "South Africa: Apartheid Military Forced Gay Troops Into Sex-Change Operations," *Thegully.com,* August 25, 2000, http://www.thegully.com/essays/africa/000825sexchange.html, (Accessed July 1, 2018).

88 C. Abayomi Cassell, *Liberia: History of the first African Republic,* (1970), p. 2.

Negro slaves had been introduced into ancient Egypt and later into Rome and the Byzantine Empire; Carthage also procured them for use in the Roman galleys. In wars of conquest in the Egyptian Sudan and along the East African coast, Arabs and Berbers had crossed the Sahara Desert from North Africa into the region of the Niger, taking slaves to southern Persia, western India, and the coasts of Arabia. Egypt, North Africa, and the Turkish Empire.

One account of how African slavery commenced in the west relates that "Henry, King of Portugal, under authority from three Roman Pontiffs" around 1454 took possession of several islands and havens on the coast of Africa; then took many slaves by force, trick, artifice, and barter.

[89] McConnaughey, Janet. "Spain's king gets key to New Orleans for 300th anniversary," *The Washington Times*, https://www.washingtontimes.com/news/2018/jun/15/spains-king-and-queen-in-new-orleans-for-300th-ann/ (Assessed June 15, 2018).

[90] Angie Debo, *A History of the Indians of the United States*, 1970, p. 6.

Discussing how Indians did not view economy or superficial achievements like the whites did ...

There was one exception in many tribes - the attainment of distinction through war honors; thus war as an exciting contest of courage, and skill was a necessity. One time in 1724 the Creeks offered to mediate between the Senecas and the Cherokees, who were having a good time collecting each other's hair, but the Senecas explained that they could not afford to make peace, "We have no people to war against nor yet no meal to eat but the Cherokees."

[91] Douglas B. Bamforth. "Indigenous People, Indigenous Violence: Pre-contact Warfare on the North American Plains," (Man., 1994), pp. 95–115.

[92]Native Languages, www.native-languages.org/iaq17.htm, Setting the record straight about native peoples: Kidnapping.

[93] Scott Zesch, *The Captured*, (New York: St. Martin's Press 2004), pp. 88–100.

[94] Northwest Ordinance of 1787.

[95] See the Homestead Act of 1862.

[96] https://www.history.com/topics/ancient-history/hammurabi.

[97] *The Holy Bible*, Genesis 6:5-8.

[98] See https://www.history.com/topics/black-history/black-codes.

Black codes were restrictive laws designed to limit the freedom of African Americans and ensure their availability as a cheap labor force after slavery was abolished during the Civil War. Though the Union victory had given some 4 million slaves their freedom, the question of freed blacks' status in the postwar South was still very much unresolved. Under black codes, many states required blacks to sign yearly labor contracts; if they refused, they risked being arrested, fined, and forced into unpaid labor. Outrage over black codes helped undermine support for President Andrew Johnson and the Republican Party.

[99] C-Span, LeeAnna Keith discusses her book *The Colfax Massacre: The Untold Story of Black Power, White Terror, and the Death of Reconstruction*, https://www.c-span.org/video/?202262-1/the-colfax-massacre.

[100] Tuskegee University, Lynchings, Whites and Negroes, 1882-1968, http://192.203.127.197/archive/bitstream/handle/123456789/511/Lyching%201882%201968.pdf.

[101] Public Broadcasting Service. "Africans in America: Fugitive Slaves and Northern Racism," http://www.pbs.org/wgbh/aia/part4/4narr3.html (Accessed May 4, 2018).

[102] Andrew Boxer, "Native Americans and the Federal Government," *Historytoday.com*, https://www.historytoday.com/andrew-boxer/native-americans-and-federal-government (Accessed May 4, 2018).

[103] John Johnson Jr., "How Los Angeles Covered Up the Massacre of 17 Chinese," *Laweekly.com*, http://www.laweekly.com/news/how-los-angeles-covered-up-the-massacre-of-17-chinese-2169478 (Accessed May 5, 2018).

[104] Gong Lum v. Rice, 275 U.S. 78 (1927).

[105] Arnold Krammer, *Undue Process: The Untold Story of America's German Alien Internees*, (Lanham, MD: Rowman & Littlefield, 1997), p. 14.

[106] Joseph D'Hippolito, "When Jerry Brown Tried to Keep Immigrants Out of California," *The Wall Street Journal*, March 9, 2018, https://www.wsj.com/articles/when-jerry-brown-tried-to-keep-immigrants-out-of-california-1520634989.

[107] See U.S. Department of Labor https://www.dol.gov/ofccp/regs/compliance/ca_11246.htm.

[108] The History Channel, Selma to Montgomery March https://www.history.com/topics/black-history/selma-montgomery-march.

[109] See CDC site https://www.cdc.gov/nchs/fastats/unmarried-childbearing.htm.

[110] Sam Gardner, "18 years later, Nykesha Sales still carries the weight of her record-breaking shot," *FOX Sports*, February 29, 2016, https://www.foxsports.com/college-basketball/story/uconn-huskies-villanova-wildcats-nykesha-sales-geno-auriemma-022916 , (Accessed September 12, 2017).

[111] Christopher Hooton, "Adele broke her Grammy award in two after saying it belonged to Beyoncé," *The Independent*, February 13, 2017, https://www.independent.co.uk/arts-entertainment/music/news/adele-grammys-2017-award-breaks-in-half-beyonce-lemonade-25-mean-girls-album-of-the-year-a7576896.html.

[112] Adam Serwer, "Lyndon Johnson was a civil rights hero. But also a racist." *MSNBC*, April 11, 2014, http://www.msnbc.com/msnbc/lyndon-johnson-civil-rights-racism, (Accessed September 21, 2017).

[113] Rupert Cornwell, "Truman diary reveals anti-Semitism and offer to step down," July 12, 2003, https://www.independent.co.uk/news/world/americas/truman-diary-reveals-anti-semitism-and-offer-to-step-down-95825.html, (Accessed September 21, 2017).

[114] Erin Nyren, "Issa Rae at the Emmys: 'I'm Rooting for Everybody Black,'" *Variety*, September 17, 2017.

[115] Michael Daniel, "Study Suggests Medical Errors Now Third Leading Cause of Death in the U.S." *Johns Hopkins Medicine Website*, https://www.hopkinsmedicine.org/news/media/releases/study_suggest s_medical_errors_now_third_leading_cause_of_death_in_the_us, (Accessed May 18, 2018).

[116] Jeremy Gorner, Jason Meisner, "FBI investigating death of teen shot 16 times by Chicago Cop," *chicagotribune.com*, *http://www.chicagotribune.com/news/ct-feds-probe-police-shooting-met-20150413-story.html*, (Accessed May 17, 2018).

[117] Quoctrung Bui and Amanda Cox, "Surprising New Evidence Shows Bias in Police Use of Force but Not in Shootings," *nytimes.com*, https://www.nytimes.com/2016/07/12/upshot/surprising-new-evidence-shows-bias-in-police-use-of-force-but-not-in-shootings.html, (Accessed May 17, 2018).

[118] Aamer Madhani, "'Ferguson effect': 72% of U.S. cops reluctant to make stops," *USA Today*, January 11, 2017.

[119] Aaron Glantz, Emmanuel Martinez, "Modern-day redlining: How banks block people of color from homeownership," *Chicago tribune*, February 15, 2018. http://www.chicagotribune.com/business/ct-biz-modern-day-redlining-20180215-story.html

[120] Sam Allard, "Cleveland Area Mortgage Lenders Are Perpetuating Redlining With Current Lending Patterns, According to Study," *clevescene.com*, July 18, 2018. https://www.clevescene.com/scene-and-heard/archives/2018/07/18/cleveland-area-mortgage-lenders-are-perpetuating-redlining-with-current-lending-patterns-according-to-study, (Accessed July 18, 2018).

[121] CBS News, "Fla. Mom gets 20 years for firing warning shots," *cbsnews.com*, https://www.cbsnews.com/news/fla-mom-gets-20-years-for-firing-warning-shots/ (Accessed June 14, 2018).

[122] See https://www.govtrack.us/congress/votes/103-1994/h416.

[123] See https://www.congress.gov/bill/99th-congress/house-bill/5484.

[124] See https://www.congress.gov/bill/100th-congress/house-bill/5210.

[125] Brian Mann, "Timeline: Black America's surprising 40-year support for the Drug War," *prisontime.com*, http://prisontime.org/2013/08/12/timeline-black-support-for-the-war-on-drugs/, (Accessed May 17, 2018).

[126] The Daily Mail, "Shocking US Government leaflet tells Mexican immigrants they can collect food stamp benefits without admitting they're in the country illegally," *dailymail.com.uk*, www.dailymail.co.uk/news/article-2315115/Shocking-US-government-leaflet-tells-Mexican-immigrants-collect-food-stamp-benefits-admitting-theyre-country-illegally.html, (Accessed, June 3 2018).

[127] Chantal Da Silva, "California school to be named after undocumented immigrant who won Pulitzer Prize," *Newsweek*, June 17, 2018.

[128] Doug Criss, "For the first time, California appoints an undocumented immigrant to state post," *CNN*, March 16, 2018.

[129] Natalie Shutler, "Cesar Vargas Is New York's First Openly Undocumented Lawyer," *Vice*, November 16, 2016, https://www.vice.com/en_us/article/5gqda3/cesar-vargas-is-new-yorks-first-openly-undocumented-lawyer-v23n8, (Accessed June 17, 2018).

[130] Ben Hill, "'We are not calling for the slaughter of white people - at least for now': South African parliament votes to SEIZE white-owned land as experts warn of violent repercussions," *Daily Mail*, February 28, 2018, http://www.dailymail.co.uk/news/article-5443599/White-South-African-farmers-removed-land.html.

[131] Tariq Tahir, "South African president vows to settle the transfer of land from white to black owners, saying: 'This sin that was committed when our country was colonised must be resolved'," *Daily Mail*, April 11, 2018. http://www.dailymail.co.uk/news/article-5450559/South-African-president-vows-transfer-land-whites-blacks.html.

[132] Christopher Woody, "These were the 50 most violent cities in the world in 2017," *BusinessInsider.com*, https://www.businessinsider.com/most-violent-cities-in-the-world-2018-3, (Accessed March 6, 2018).

[133] Fabiola Zerpa, "In Venezuela, a Haircut Costs 5 Bananas and 2 Eggs," *Bloomberg.com*, https://www.bloomberg.com/news/articles/2018-05-04/in-caracus-venezuela-a-haircut-costs-five-bananas-and-two-eggs, (Accessed May 4, 2018).

[134] Jared Bernstein, "Why Seattle 'Head Tax' is relevant to the nation" *Chicago Tribune*, May 16, 2018. http://www.chicagotribune.com/news/opinion/commentary/ct-perspec-seattle-head-tax-20180516-story.html.

[135] Nereida Moreno. "Ald. Pawar Wants Chicago To Try Universal Basic Income," *wbez.org* https://www.wbez.org/shows/morning-shift/ald-pawar-wants-chicago-to-try-universal-basic-income/0d205ad0-457e-4682-8d80-7e2b0059d1a9, (Accessed July 25, 2018).

[136] Wal-Mart 2018 Annual Report, http://www.corporatereport.com/walmart/2018/ar/

[137] Julia Horowitz. "Walmart's CEO earns 1,188 times as much as the company's median worker," *money.cnn.com* https://money.cnn.com/2018/04/23/news/companies/walmart-ceo-pay/index.html, (Accessed April 23, 2018).

[138] New York Times Archives, "The Right Minimum Wage: $0.00," *The New York Times*, https://www.nytimes.com/1987/01/14/opinion/the-right-minimum-wage-0.00.html, (Accessed April 23, 2018).

[139] Buz Humphrey, "Minimum-wage mandate will hurt my disabled son's prospects," *The Seattle Times*, June 1, 2018, https://www.seattletimes.com/opinion/minimum-wage-mandate-will-hurt-my-disabled-sons-prospects/.

[140] *Tucker Carlson Tonight*, Mike Rowe's take: Man-babies, Starbucks 'Shelters' and 'safe spaces,' http://video.foxnews.com/v/5789429893001/?#sp=show-clips, (Accessed May 24, 2018).

[141] Dan Holly, "The Truck stops here," *miamitimesonline.com*, http://www.miamitimesonline.com/business/the-truck-stops-

here/article_b83b993e-91ae-11e8-a28f-a3455b3fa926.html (Accessed July 27, 2018).

142 David Wren, "Here's why thousands of good-paying jobs go unfilled in South Carolina," *postandcourier.com* https://www.postandcourier.com/business/here-s-why-thousands-of-good-paying-jobs-go-unfilled/article_8e901a7e-53a6-11e8-b512-ab3a41a9133e.html (Accessed May 12, 2018).

143 Associated Press, "Officials: Thousands of Idaho skilled jobs go unfilled," *spokesman.com* http://www.spokesman.com/stories/2018/jan/18/officials-thousands-of-idaho-skilled-jobs-go-unfil/ (Accessed January 18, 2018).

144 Enjoli commercial, https://youtu.be/_UIktO4Pnlw.

145 https://www.congress.gov/bill/103rd-congress/house-bill/1793.

146 https://cte.ed.gov/legislation/about-perkins-iv.

147 https://www2.ed.gov/about/offices/list/ocr/docs/tix_dis.html.

148 Dr. Michael W. Kirst, "Women Earn More Degrees Than Men; Gap Keeps Increasing," *Stanford.edu*, May 28, 2013, https://collegepuzzle.stanford.edu/tag/women-exceed-men-in-college-graduation/.

149 Christopher Cornwell et al., "Non-cognitive Skills and the Gender Disparities in Test Scores and Teacher Assessments: Evidence from Primary School," *Journal of Social Resources*, Winter, 2013, pp. 26–264.

150 Christina Hoff Sommers, *The War on Boys*, (New York: Simon & Schuster, 2013), p. 39.

151 Ibid., pp. 64–65.

152 Amber Athey, "Sen. Gillibrand: 'Lehman Sisters' might not have caused financial collapse," *The Daily Caller*, May 15, 2018.

153 Breanna Edwards, "'Men Have Been Getting On My Nerves Lately': Barack Obama, Forever a Mood, Speaks Out For the Empowerment of Women in South Africa," *The Root*, July 19, 2018, https://www.theroot.com/men-have-been-getting-on-my-nerves-lately-barack-obama-1827714989.

154 Glenn Kessler. "President Obama's persistent '77-cent' claim on the wage gap gets a new Pinocchio rating," *The Washington Post*, https://www.washingtonpost.com/news/fact-checker/wp/2014/04/09/president-obamas-persistent-77-cent-claim-on-the-wage-gap-gets-a-new-pinocchio-rating/?utm_term=.8d02d3cecf94 (Accessed June 3, 2018).

155 Glenn Kessler. "The 'Equal Pay Day' factoid that women make 78 cents for every dollar earned by men," *The Washington Post*, https://www.washingtonpost.com/news/fact-checker/wp/2015/04/02/the-equal-pay-day-factoid-that-women-make-78-cents-for-every-dollar-earned-by-men/?utm_term=.21926e05aedf (Accessed June 3, 2018).

156 Robert J. Samuelson. "What is the real gender pay gap?" *The Washington Post*, https://www.washingtonpost.com/opinions/whats-the-real-gender-pay-gap/2016/04/24/314a90ee-08a1-11e6-bdcb-0133da18418d_story.html?utm_term=.b9b31cc45bde (Accessed April 12, 2018).

157 Jennifer Lawrence, "Why Do I Make Less Than My Male Co-Stars?," *lennyletter.com*, October 13, 2015, https://www.lennyletter.com/story/jennifer-lawrence-why-do-i-make-less-than-my-male-costars, (Accessed April 12, 2018).

158 Andrea Mandell, "Exclusive: Wahlberg got $1.5M for 'All the Money' reshoot, Williams paid less than $1,000," *USAtoday.com*, January 9, 2018. https://www.usatoday.com/story/life/people/2018/01/09/exclusive-wahlberg-paid-1-5-m-all-money-reshoot-williams-got-less-than-1-000/1018351001/.

159 Robert J. Samuelson, "What's the Real Gender Pay Gap?", *The Washington Post*, April 24, 2016, https://www.washingtonpost.com/opinions/whats-the-real-gender-pay-gap/2016/04/24/314a90ee-08a1-11e6-bdcb-0133da18418d_story.html?utm_term=.c2e489b9460e, (Accessed April 12, 2018).

[160] Iris Bohnet, *What Works: Gender Equality by Design.* (London: The Belknap Press, 2016), p. 134.

[161] Christopher P. Krebs, Et al. (2007). *The Campus Sexual Assault (CSA) Study.*
Retrieved from National Criminal Justice Reference Service Website: https://www.ncjrs.gov/pdffiles1/nij/grants/221153.pdf.

[162] David Cantor et al. (2015). *Report on the AAU Campus Climate Survey on Sexual Assault and Sexual Misconduct.*
Retrieved from Association of American Universities website: https://www.aau.edu/sites/default/files/%40%20Files/Climate%20Survey/AAU_Campus_Climate_Survey_12_14_15.pdf.

[163] Hal Dardick, "Alderman to Chick-fil-A: No Deal," *Chicago Tribune*, July 25, 2012, www.chicagotribune.com/business/ct-met-chicago-chick-fil-a-20120725-story.html, (Accessed April 9, 2018).

[164] Emanuella Grinberg, "Planet Fitness revokes woman's membership after transgender complaint," *CNN*, March 9, 2015, https://www.cnn.com/2015/03/07/living/feat-planet-fitness-transgender-member/index.html, (Accessed April 12, 2018).

[165] Virginia Valian, *Why so Slow? The Advancement of Women*, (Cambridge, MA: MIT Press, 1999), p. 13.

[166] Sherie Ryder, Chimamanda Ngozi Adichie: "Changing men and opening doors," *BBC News*, June 8, 2018.

[167] Ashifa Kassam, et al., "Europe needs many more babies to avert a population disaster," *The Guardian.com*, https://www.theguardian.com/world/2015/aug/23/baby-crisis-europe-brink-depopulation-disaster (Accessed April 9, 2018).

[168] David Weiner, "Russell Crowe: People Will be Surprised by 'Noah,'" *etonline.com*, https://www.etonline.com/movies/134773_Russell_Crowe_Talks_Noah (Accessed February 12, 2018).

[169] Carol Kuruvilla, "5 Things You Need To Know About Sharia Law," *Huffpost*, January 31, 2017,

https://www.huffingtonpost.com/entry/5-facts-you-need-to-know-about-sharia-law_us_5788f567e4b03fc3ee507c01.

170 Cassandra Vinograd, Alastair Jamieson, et.al, "Charlie Hebdo Shooting: 12 killed at Muhammad Cartoons Magazine in Paris," *NBC News*, January 7, 2015, https://www.nbcnews.com/storyline/paris-magazine-attack/charlie-hebdo-shooting-12-killed-muhammad-cartoons-magazine-paris-n281266, (Accessed March 3, 2018).

171 Daniel Howden. "'Don't kill me,' she screamed. Then they stoned her to death," *The Independent*, November 9, 2008, https://www.independent.co.uk/news/world/africa/dont-kill-me-she-screamed-then-they-stoned-her-to-death-1003462.html (Accessed February 15, 2018).

172 Gul Tuysuz, What is Sharia Law?" *CNN*, August 16, 2016,https://www.cnn.com/2016/08/16/world/sharia-law-definition/index.html, (Accessed March 3, 2018).

173 Hayley Gleeson and Julie Baird, "I'm not his property: Abused Muslim women denied right to divorce," *abc.net.au*, April 18, 2018, http://mobile.abc.net.au/news/2018-04-18/abused-muslim-women-denied-right-to-divorce/9632772.

174 Mohammed Jamjoom, "Saudi Arabia issues warning against women's driving campaign," *CNN*, October 24, 2013, https://www.cnn.com/2013/10/24/world/meast/saudi-arabia-women-drivers/index.html, (Accessed May 12, 2018).

175 Saroop Ijaz, "'Honor' killings continue in Pakistan despite new law," *Human Rights Watch*, March, 1 2018.

176 Paul Harris and Ewen MacAskill, "US midterm election results herald new political era as Republicans take House," *The Guardian*, November 3, 2010, https://www.theguardian.com/world/2010/nov/03/us-midterm-election-results-tea-party, (Accessed February 15, 2018).

177 Edward-Isaac Dovere and John Bresnahan, "How the Democrats lost the Senate," *politico.com*, November, 11, 2014,

https://www.politico.com/story/2014/11/democrats-lose-2014-midterms-112581, (Accessed February 15, 2018).

[178] Brent Budowsky, "George Will, Joe Scarborough lead midterm exodus from GOP," *The Hill*, July, 6, 2018, http://thehill.com/opinion/campaign/395767-george-will-joe-scarborough-lead-midterm-exodus-from-gop.

[179] 270 to win.

[180] The Associated Press, "NYC to send volunteers to legal assistance effort at border," *New Jersey Herald*, July 30, 2018.

[181] Katie Martin, "How the Left Lost Its Mind," *The Atlantic*, July 2, 2017, https://www.theatlantic.com/politics/archive/2017/07/liberal-fever-swamps/530736/, (Accessed July 18, 2018).

[182] Lindsey Bever and Herman Wong, "'I hope Trump is assassinated': A Missouri lawmaker faces mounting calls to resign after Facebook comment," *The Washington Post*, August 18, 2017.

[183] Brad Heath, "Baltimore police stopped noticing crime after Freddie Gray's death. A wave of killings followed," USA Today, July 12, 2018, https://www.usatoday.com/story/news/nation/2018/07/12/baltimore-police-not-noticing-crime-after-freddie-gray-wave-killings-followed/744741002/.

[184] Julie Compton, "Boy or girl? Parents raising 'theybies' let kids decide," *NBC News*, (July 19, 2018).

[185] Jessica Bies, "Regulation would let students "self-identify" gender, race without parental OK,", *The News Journal*, November 13, 2017.

[186] Emily Foxhall, "Complaint: Katy-area teacher fired for refusing to address girl, 6, as transgender boy," *Houston Chronicle,* November, 10, 2015, https://www.chron.com/neighborhood/katy/news/article/Attorneys-Katy-area-teacher-fired-for-refusing-6622339.php, (Accessed June 28, 2018).

[187] Hans Fiene, "Ask Hillary Clinton Why Abortion Is A 'Difficult Decision,'" *The Federalist*, April 8, 2016.

188 Peter Beinart, "How the Democrats Lost Their Way on Immigration," *The Atlantic*,https://www.theatlantic.com/magazine/archive/2017/07/the-democrats-immigration-mistake/528678/ (Accessed June 28, 2018).

189 See https://votesmart.org/public-statement/435424/remarks-by-us-senator-charles-e-schumer-6th-annual-immigration-law-and-policy-conference-migration-policy-institute#.W0azMiNOnpE (Accessed June 28, 2018).

190 Seth McLaughlin, "Hillary: Illegal immigrant children must be sent home," *washingtontimes.com*, https://m.washingtontimes.com/news/2014/jun/17/hillary-illegal-immigrant-children-must-be-sent-ho/ (Accessed June 28, 2018).

191 Snopes Fact Check, "Did the Obama Administration Place Immigrant Children with Human Traffickers?" *Snopes.com*, July, 2018, https://www.snopes.com/fact-check/did-obama-administration-children-human-traffickers/.

192 Caleb Howe, Obama DHS Sec. Jeh Johnson 'Freely Admits' They Detained Children, Families: 'We Believed It Was Necessary'," *Mediaite.com*, June 24, 2018, https://www.mediaite.com/tv/obama-dhs-sec-jeh-johnson-freely-admits-they-detained-children-families-we-believed-it-was-necessary/.

193 Elizabeth A. Harris, "De Blasio Proposes Changes to New York's Elite High Schools," *The New York Times*, June 2, 2018, https://www.nytimes.com/2018/06/02/nyregion/de-blasio-new-york-schools.html.

194 Lauren Rearick, "Emma Stone's Oscars 2018 Introduction of the Best Director Category Faces Backlash," *teenvogue.com*, https://www.teenvogue.com/story/emma-stone-oscars-2018-introduction-white-feminism (Accessed March 5, 2018).

195 Alex Harris, "Black Marjory Stoneman Douglas students want the movement to include their voices too," *Miami Herald*, March 29, 2018,

https://www.miamiherald.com/news/local/community/broward/artic
le207251449.html.

[196] Jeff Cimmino, "University of Chicago Professor: Infanticide Is Morally
Acceptable," *National Review*, July 19, 2017,
https://www.nationalreview.com/2017/07/infanticide-morally-
acceptable-professor-argues/, (Accessed July 21, 2018).

[197] Ellen Barry and Martin Selsoe Sorensen, "In Denmark, Harsh New
Laws for Immigrant 'Ghettos'," *The New York Times*, July 2, 2018,
https://www.nytimes.com/2018/07/01/world/europe/denmark-
immigrant-ghettos.html.

[198] Agence France-Presse, "First woman fined in Demark for wearing full-
face veil," *The Guardian*, August 3, 2018,
https://www.theguardian.com/world/2018/aug/04/first-woman-fined-
in-denmark-for-wearing-full-face-veil.

[199] Michael Sigman, "For Mitt, Firing People Is the Context," *Huffpost*,
March 16, 2012, https://www.huffingtonpost.com/michael-
sigman/mitt-romney-firing-people_b_1207525.html, (Accessed July
30, 2018).

[200] Amy Davidson Sorkin, "Mitt's binders and the missing women," *The
New Yorker*, October 16, 2012,
https://www.newyorker.com/news/daily-comment/mitts-binders-and-
the-missing-women, (Accessed July 30, 2018).

[201] Phillip Rucker, "Mitt Romney's dog-on-the-car-roof story still proves to
be his critics' best friend," *The Washington Post*, March 14, 2012,
https://www.washingtonpost.com/politics/mitt-romneys-dog-on-the-
car-roof-story-still-proves-to-be-his-critics-best-
friend/2012/03/14/gIQAp2LxCS_story.html?utm_term=.9cd8e8f3250
7, (Accessed July 31, 2018).

[202] Jason Horowitz, "Mitt Romney's prep school classmates recall pranks,
but also troubling incidents," *The Washington Post*, May 11, 2012,
https://www.washingtonpost.com/politics/mitt-romneys-prep-school-
classmates-recall-pranks-but-also-troubling-

incidents/2012/05/10/gIQA3WOKFU_story.html?utm_term=.c68345 541b86, (Accessed July 31, 2018).

[203] Mark McKinnon, "Tax Chat, felon, murderer: meet Mitt Romney, if Barack Obama's backers are to be believed," *The Telegraph*, August, 2012, https://www.telegraph.co.uk/news/worldnews/mitt-romney/9469242/Tax-cheat-felon-murderer-meet-Mitt-Romney-if-Barack-Obamas-backers-are-to-be-believed.html, (Accessed July 31, 2018).

[204] Aaron Goldstein, "George W. Bush, Liberals' New Hero," *The National Review*, March 6, 2017, https://www.nationalreview.com/2017/03/george-w-bush-liberals-freedom-press-media-russia-investigation-donald-trump/, (Accessed August 1, 2018).

[205] Michael Janofsky, "The 2004 Campaign Advertising; Bush-Hitler Ads Draw Criticism," *The New York Times*, January 6, 2004, https://www.nytimes.com/2004/01/06/us/the-2004-campaign-advertising-bush-hitler-ads-draw-criticism.html , (*NYTimes* Archives: August 1, 2018).

[206] Declan McCullagh, "McCain's 'Bomb Iran' song was anti-Muslim?" *cnet.com*, April 22, 2007, https://www.cnet.com/news/oneplus-6t-will-launch-in-october-with-t-mobile-as-us-partner/, (Accessed August 1, 2018).

[207] Win McCormack, "100 Reasons to Vote Against John McCain," *Huffpost*, December 4, 2008, https://www.huffingtonpost.com/win-mccormack/100-reasons-to-vote-again_b_140627.html, (Accessed August 1, 2018).

[208] Joe Cutbirth, "McCain's Racist Surge," *Huffpost*, November 15, 2008, https://www.huffingtonpost.com/joe-cutbirth/mccains-racist-surge_b_134868.html, (Accessed August 1, 2018).

[209] Christian Gollayan, "Swimsuit model breastfeeds on the catwalk," *The New York Post*, July 16, 2018.

210 Bill Barrow and Chevel Johnson, "Warren: Criminal justice system 'racist' ...'front to back'," *AP News*, August 4, 2018, https://apnews.com/bc50cc6f4a864bc790c2226fe29a5f21.

211 Bonobos, #EvolveTheDefinition, https://www.youtube.com/watch?v=j6jz2Jma5-s&feature=youtu.be.

Made in the
USA
Columbia, SC